The Land of Lost Content

The landscape of A E Housman's *A Shropshire Lad* and *Collected Poems*;
its farms, its spires, valleys and folded hills

by Jane Allsopp

Shropshire Books

The Land of Lost Content

Front Cover: St. Laurence's Church, Ludlow
© Jane Allsopp 1995
ISBN: 0-903802-66-X
Cover and book design: Paul Brasenell
Managing Editor: Helen Sample

Published by Shropshire Books,
the publishing division of Shropshire County Council's
Information & Community Services Department.

Printed in Great Britain by Livesey Limited, Shrewsbury.

Contents

Into my heart an air that kills
From yon far country blows:
What are those blue remembered hills,
What spires, what farms are those?

That is the land of lost content,
I see it shining plain,
The happy highways where I went
And cannot come again.

A Shropshire Lad, XL
A E Housman

Preface

When I was four, my parents took on an empty cottage, with doors that had warped and windows that had cracked and with a garden and orchard that nature had very firmly reclaimed as her own. To get through the garden gate the neighbouring farmer's son flourished the shears and hacked the holly and hawthorn back so that my mother, father and he could squeeze through the thicket. The front door failed to yield by turn of the key, so the toe of his boot finally gained access. The corn was higher than I was that harvest time.

This was nine miles from Ludlow on a hillside that offered vistas of South Shropshire's most ravishing scenery - Wenlock Edge, Clun Forest, the Long Mynd, Abdon Burf, Clee Liberty, the Teme valley and the Corvedale. It was so remote that it was, and still is, a mile from the nearest made-up road. But I began to grow up in this isolated, and very rural, corner of South Shropshire with Ludlow as our market town.

As I grew, I began to read and to love A E Housman's poems, *A Shropshire Lad*, and his other verse. As my appreciation of his verse grew, I realised just how much they evoked the spirit and presence of this border land county with its valleys and hills, hamlets and farms. The centenary of the publication of *A Shropshire Lad* seemed a fitting time to write about the Shropshire of Housman's verse and this particular corner of the county which I have come to love so much.

So the inspiration and motivation to write this book was twofold: first the land of south Shropshire itself - its very rural market towns, woodlands and farmsteads with their orchards, secondly A E Housman's poetry, wherein these valleys and hills have been immortalised. As long as I have known Housman's poetry it has always seemed to me that what I saw before me in the Shropshire landscape was what I also heard in the poetry. This book is a small attempt to show, in my very personal view, how the two are irretrievably linked.

And so this is very firmly not a biography of Housman. It is an evocation of the real land that inspired his poetry so the reader will find little of Housman's life and story in a biographical sense here. It will, I hope, go a small way to give a feeling for his *"land of lost content"*.

Linked with my description of the landscape, villages and churchyards of South Shropshire, I have quoted from A E Housman's *A Shropshire Lad* and *Collected Poems*. The poems I have chosen are those which to me seem to capture the very essence, atmosphere and spirit of this land.

Jane M Allsopp
July 1994

A Map of Housman's Shropshire

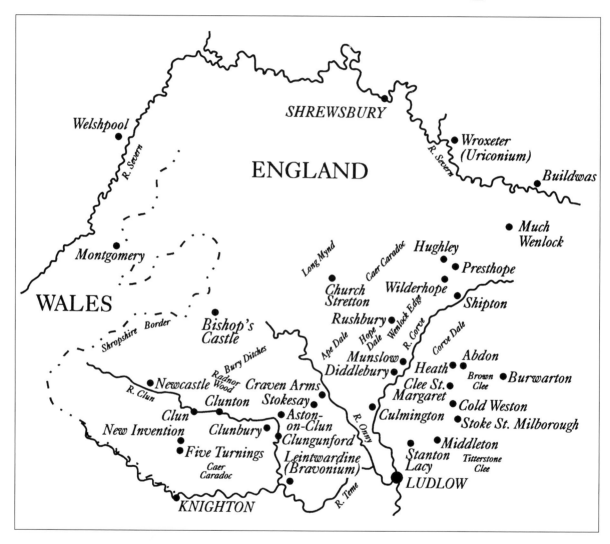

The land of A. E. Housman's A Shropshire Lad and Collected Poems -
the rivers, valleys, towns and hills

The Poems

The poems are taken from the edition which I have always used and read -
the Jonathan Cape edition, which was the first definitive edition
of Housman's collected poetry.

Legend

Throughout the book where A E Housman's poems are quoted ASL, LP, MP and AP
refer to *A Shropshire Lad*, *Last Poems*, *More Poems* and *Additional Poems* respectively.
The Roman numerals refer to the number of the poems
as they appear in complete editions.

The Land of Lost Content

For those who inspired me to write
this book -

Jack Clee, late of Sutton Hill, Stanton Lacy;
My parents, who brought me first to Ludlow;
and my husband.

Joy, take my hand, talk to my heart,

Fold here awhile your wings and stay.

Soon but not yet must we depart

To west and east away.

(The original first stanza of
Tarry, delight, so seldɔm met
but eventually not used by AEH)

Chapter One

What Are Those Blue Remembered Hills?

Many times I have been asked 'what was Housman's connection with Shropshire?
Why did he he write particularly about Clun, Clee and Ludlow?'

It would not be unjust to Housman to answer those questions simply by saying it was the distant view of the Shropshire hills from his childhood home that gave the initial inspiration.

Housman himself confirmed this very simple answer in letters written long after *A Shropshire Lad* had been first published. In a letter dated 14 April 1934 to Houston Martin, (a youthful early American devotee of *A Shropshire Lad*), who had also asked 'why Shropshire?', Housman had simply answered "Shropshire was our western horizon, which made me feel romantic about it". Again, in a letter to Maurice Pullet of 5 February 1933 he wrote "I had a sentimental feeling for Shropshire because its hills were our western horizon".

The Housman family home was at Bromsgrove, Worcestershire, some forty miles from the South Shropshire border. It is well known that Alfred Edward, first as a child then as a young man, would climb the little hill outside their home, Perry Hall, and gaze westward to the Shropshire hills. From this point in Bromsgrove the western horizon is bordered by the two high Shropshire peaks of Brown Clee and Titterstone Clee, beyond them is the Welsh border. Over these hills the sun sets on its western course, giving the impression that they really do appear to be surrounded by a blue haze.

Brown Clee Hill

When summer's end is nighing
And skies at evening cloud,
I muse on change and fortune
And all the feats I vowed
When I was young and proud.

The weathercock at sunset
Would lose the slanted ray,
And I would climb the beacon
That looked to Wales away
And saw the last of day.

From hill and cloud and heaven
The hues of evening died;
Night welled through lane and hollow
And hushed the countryside,
But I had youth and pride.

And I with earth and nightfall
In converse high would stand,
Late, till the west was ashen
And darkness hard at hand,
And the eye lost the land.

The year might age, and cloudy
The lessening day might close,
But air of other summers
Breathed from beyond the snows,
And I had hope of those.

They came and were and are not
And come no more anew;
And all the years and seasons
That ever can ensue
Must now be worse and few.

So here's an end of roaming
On eves when autumn nighs:
The ear too fondly listens
For summer's parting sighs,
And then the heart replies.

LPXXXIX

Born in 1859 at Fockbury, near Bromsgrove, in Worcestershire, the eldest son of a provincial Worcestershire solicitor, Housman attended the local public school, Bromsgrove School. He went on to Oxford, but failed in Greats, the Final School examination, and so left there without a degree. He then went to work at the Patent Office in London in 1882 but by 1892 his hours of application, dedication, and translation and study of Latin texts lead him to be successfully considered for the post of Professor of Latin at University College, London. It was largely during these early years at University College, London, that Housman wrote the verse that was to become known as *A Shropshire Lad*. He suffered as all who aspire to have their words published in the difficulty of not finding a willing publisher for his poems and the first edition of A Shropshire Lad was published privately at his expense in 1896. It has never since been out of print during the past one hundred years!

His Latin and Greek scholarship, meantime, was becoming increasingly esteemed and respected and in 1911 he became Professor of Latin at Cambridge, a post he held until his death in 1936. He was a meticulous stickler for accuracy, facts and correctness and I am strongly tempted to believe that the fame of his supposed off-handedness was used as an excuse by those who fell short of his own demanding standards. I think he was probably someone whom we today would describe as one who did not suffer fools gladly.

Throughout his life and without exception, Housman kept his scholarship and academic work totally separate from his own creative writing of poetry. He published his last collection of verse, *Last Poems*, in 1922. It is to Housman's brother Laurence (with whom he kept up affectionate and lively correspondence during term time at London and Cambridge) that we owe the posthumous publication of a further two collections of poems. A E Housman's *More Poems* and *Additional Poems* were published by his brother Laurence in 1936 and 1937 respectively.

It was the stringent academic standards which Housman set himself, coupled with the insular and isolated backdrop of the University walls at Cambridge, that has probably done more to enhance his reputation as something of a lone, single bachelor who was difficult and a recluse. That his father had subjected Alfred as a young boy to circumcision must surely have left an emotional scarring which undoubtedly contributed to an adult life of repressed emotions. That also throughout his life ran a thread of sadness and melancholy because of unfulfilled relationships there is no doubt, and this is nowhere more clearly visible than in his later poems.

But it is his evocation of Shropshire, its southern hills, valleys, that also endures. Today at Ludlow May Fair, or on Monday morning at the market in Ludlow, the spirit of *A Shropshire Lad* is conjured anew. As the chimes ring down 'The Conquering Hero' once more, as they have done for years, or the banks of the Teme are brim full of mist, Housman's words, for me at least, strike at the very spirit of the place. And it is always Housman's vision which fills the void of Ludlow tower at the Parish Church of St Laurence's when on each Remembrance Sunday the town stands in silence waiting for the great bell of the tower to strike the hour. He is gone, with the lads who will not return, but his memorial is here at Ludlow. He sought no honours during his life time and even refused the Order of Merit. I have a belief he would wish no other honour than his memorial on Ludlow church to be caught every evening by the last rays of the sun as it sinks in the west below Wenlock Edge.

Housman's mother had obviously told her children of Shropshire and left a fond image of the county in Alfred Edward's heart. In later life Housman recalled his mother's memories of the county in the mid-nineteenth century. In 1896 Housman wrote to his brother Laurence, "I was in Bridgnorth for several hours. In the churchyard there I remembered having heard our mother describe it and the steps up to it, which I had absolutely forgotten for more than twenty five years." His mother's death in 1871, on Alfred's twelfth birthday, seems to stand as a catalyst of sadness in what was largely thereafter to be a life of repressed emotions and a longing to return to a land that was always just out of reach beyond the horizon.

Much of it still out of easy reach of the commuter today, Shropshire at the turn of the century was indeed a land cut off from towns of the relatively near industrial midlands and a far, far distance from London. So this wild upland with remote hamlets by falling streams and standing hills became for Housman a vision of perfect unspoilt rural England, but it is countryside where suffering and pain are felt as much by lads in Knighton as those in London. The only difference is that the countryside's beauty is a palliative for the ills the lads of Knighton and Ludlow suffer.

Housman had started to write some of the verse that was to become *A Shropshire Lad* when in November 1894 his father died. The death of his father obviously necessitated a visit back from London to his Bromsgrove home for the funeral and the completion of family arrangements. The next few months were to produce some of the best poems of *A Shropshire Lad* and the time was described by Housman as "my most prolific period, the first five months of 1895".

After the funeral of his father Housman stayed on for some time at the family home in Bromsgrove. It was at this time, over the winter and early spring of 1894-95, that Housman took advantage of being back in the area to visit Shropshire "to gain local colour", as he put it, for his poems. There was a good railway service into Ludlow and on to Knighton beyond at that time and a line which ran across Wenlock Edge was only closed in 1962. We can piece together a little of his journeys into South Shropshire at this time because of these railway routes of the time and from some of Housman's own notes.

It has been a constant source of academic argument as to how often Housman actually came to Shropshire and how well he knew the county. We know that he owned a copy of the 1879 edition of 'A Handbook to Shropshire, Cheshire and Lancashire' by J Murray. We know too, from letters to his brother Laurence, that he did visit the county on several occasions whilst writing *A Shropshire Lad*. It has often seemed to me that many academics have overlooked the ease with which Housman could have travelled around south Shropshire at this time. Railway lines existed to remote corners of the county then, and it is of these corners of which he writes - and with an astonishing degree of topographical accuracy to my mind. From Ludlow the railway ran to Knighton, down the Clun and Onny valleys with a station at Clungunford; it ran across Wenlock Edge, down past Buildwas under the Wrekin and into Much Wenlock. There were also two lines that ran to the two Clee Hills - Titterstone and the other up to Brown Clee Hill, Ditton Priors, at Abdon under Clee.

As through the wild green hills of Wyre

The train ran, changing sky and shire,

And far behind, a fading crest,

Low in the forsaken west

Sank the high-reared head of Clee,

My hand lay empty on my knee.

Aching on my knee it lay:

That morning half a shire away

So many an honest fellow's fist

Had well-nigh wrung it from the wrist.

Hand, said I, since now we part

From fields and men we know by heart,

For strangers' faces, strangers' lands,

Hand, you have held true fellows' hands.

Be clean then; rot before you do

A thing they'd not believe of you.

You and I must keep from shame

In London streets the Shropshire name;

On banks of Thames they must not say

Severn breeds worse men than they;

And friends abroad must bear in mind

Friends at home they leave behind.

Oh, I shall be stiff and cold

When I forget you, hearts of gold;

The land where I shall mind you not

Is the land where all's forgot.

And if my foot returns no more

To Teme nor Corve nor Severn shore,

Luck, my lads, be with you still

By falling stream and standing hill,

By chiming tower and whispering tree,

Men that made a man of me.

About your work in town and farm

Still you'll keep my head from harm,

Still you'll help me, hands that gave

A grasp to friend me to the grave.

ASL XXXVII

The line from Worcestershire, Housman's native county, ran via Bewdley into Shropshire, passing through the west midlands' last great remaining sweep of ancient woodland, the Wyre Forest, presenting views across to the gateway into Housman's particular corner of South Shropshire. The wooded valleys run down before the ground sweeps up to the two guardians of the south-west Shropshire border, Titterstone and Brown Clee Hills. For those of us approaching this area of Shropshire today by road, a sublime transition occurs when the summit of Titterstone Clee has been reached from across the upland barren heights - with incredible panoramas stretching out over at least seven counties ranging from Edge Hill in Gloucestershire to the Brecon Beacons in south Wales and beyond - until a corner is turned at the top of the hill and all of Housman's Shropshire is laid before you: Ludlow and its tower; Wenlock Edge; the Wrekin; Clun Forest; the Welsh uplands beyond Knighton and all enfolded by rolling, wooded hills with streams and rivers flowing down eventually to meet the Severn.

In October 1896 we know from letters to his brother Laurence that Housman had been in South Shropshire. His letter records how he stood on Wenlock Edge: a figure, gazing down above Roman Bank, then into Corvedale and towards Ludlow, then looking north to Hughley, north to Buildwas and the Severn with the Wrekin behind, and west, always west, towards Clun, the road to Wales and the setting sun.

Housman's first collection of poems, *A Shropshire Lad*, was published in 1896. After this time his visits to South Shropshire became more random. Probably having committed his Shropshire lad's thoughts to print, and having made those important visits of which we know so little to his favourite corner of the county in the winter and spring of 1895, my own suspicion is that he then wanted to keep this memory of his land of lost content safe from harm. He did not want to see it sullied with life's bitter experiences. The poetry is full of references to the "happy highways where I went and cannot come again"; "if my foot returns no more"; "The wind and I, we both were there, but neither long abode". It was as though Housman had deliberately decided to leave this 1895 vision of South Shropshire engraved on his heart and memory for ever and not to return. They had brought back memories of a fleeting, happy childhood when his mother was alive and had first told him of Shropshire, they encapsulated the world before it was devastated by the 1914-18 war, they told of a corner of England whose way of life was largely unchanged since the Mortimers and Tudors had ruled the land. Hands that had held true fellows' hands would not return to shake them again. Time had moved on, and life's bitter experience was now worn into the lines on those hands. He would not take that bitter experience back to the land that had given him such contentment. However, as his health began to fail him during the last two years of his life he obviously felt a desire to return to his land of lost content. His brother, Laurence, recorded in his memoirs: "Fortunately during his last two years I was able to arrange that we should take holidays together; and in the summer of 1934, staying at Droitwich, only six miles from our old home, we made long motor-rounds daily through Worcestershire, Gloucestershire, Herefordshire and Shropshire."

This book is not intended to tell of the deeper significance of Housman's verse; of the dual role that the lad from Shropshire plays - the one who drinks in Ludlow ale houses, ploughs with his team and comes in for the May fair; and the other who grasps the stinging nettles of life with his bare hands, either ending his life by choice or is killed far from Shropshire in foreign fields. It is about the places of this corner of rural England on its border with Wales in which Housman chose to set his verse and which are so vital to it.

Chapter Two

By Hanging Woods and Hamlets - Upper Corvedale

The Merry Guide

Once in the wind of morning
I ranged the thymy wold;
The world-wide air was azure
And all the brooks ran gold.

There through the dews beside me
Behold a youth that trod,
With feathered cap on forehead,
And poised a golden rod.

With mien to match the morning
And gay delightful guise
And friendly brows and laughter
He looked me in the eyes.

Oh whence, I asked, and whither?
He smiled and would not say,
And looked at me and beckoned
And laughed and led the way.

And with kind looks and laughter
And naught to say beside
We two went on together,
I and my happy guide.

Across the glittering pastures
And empty upland still
And solitude of shepherds
High in the folded hill,

By hanging woods and hamlets
That gaze through orchards down
On many a windmill turning
And far-discovered town,

With gay regards of promise
And sure unslackened stride
And smiles and nothing spoken
Led on my merry guide.

By blowing realms of woodland
With sunstruck vanes afield
And cloud-led shadows sailing
About the windy weald,

By valley-guarded granges
And silver waters wide,
Content at heart I followed
With my delightful guide.

And like the cloudy shadows
Across the country blown
We two fare on for ever,
But not we two alone.

With the great gale we journey
That breathes from gardens thinned,
Borne in the drift of blossoms
Whose petals throng the wind;

Buoyed on the heaven-heard whisper
Of dancing leaflets whirled
From all the woods that autumn
Bereaves in all the world.

And midst the fluttering legion
Of all that ever died
I follow, and before us
Goes the delightful guide,

With lips that brim with laughter
But never once respond,
And feet that fly on feathers,
And serpent-circled wand.

ASL XLII

Brown Clee Hill in the distance with the eastern high ground
of Corvedale - the land of deserted medieval villages.

Remote Abdon Church with its semi-circular churchyard
enclosed with ancient yews. They suggest a pre-Christian site.

Cold Weston Hill looking into Wales.
"West and away from here to heaven, Still is the land".

The fading crest of the high-reared head of Clee
just visible to the left of Bitterley church's tower.

"The night is freezing fast, To-morrow comes December; And winterfalls of old Are with me from the past;"

The church of St. Mary, Cold Weston. A first record was made of the village in 1090; by 1341 it was deserted. The church survived in use until 1980.

Helgot the Norman's stronghold now still occupied as part
of a working farm at Holdgate in Corvedale.

By Hanging Woods and Hamlets
- Upper Corvedale

"In the southern half of the county, to which I have confined myself, the hills are generally long ridges running from north to south, with valleys, broad or narrow, between".

So Housman described the land in which Corvedale lies.

The Corvedale valley stretches between Ludlow and Much Wenlock - two medieval towns who jealously seem to guard the dale - and for whom many centuries appear to have passed by without much note.

There are two main routes which run up and down the dale from south to north. One is the main road now running through Corvedale immediately under the eastern escarpment of Wenlock Edge and the other, the old ancient medieval highway through Peaton, Bouldon, Tugford and Holdgate. A higher road runs parallel to Wenlock Edge on the opposite hillside. This lane runs above the dale to the wild, remote lands of deserted medieval villages, Iron Age forts, and tiny hamlets separated by ancient, deep green lanes, streams (called "dingles" in this part of the country) ancient woodland and Norman chapels. The names of these tiny settlements are redolent of rural and Anglo Saxon England - Hayton's Bent, Abdon, Witchcot and Postons.

The Clee Hills, to the west of Ludlow, rise up from the high ground of Whitbach, just outside Ludlow. Brown Clee forms a high vision on this eastern boundary of Corvedale, blocking the view east. The lane from Whitbach rises quickly and steeply onto the first escarpment which forms a plinth on which Brown Clee sits above the River Corve. The land eventually becomes a high ridge at the wild, rather lonely, crossroads of Hayton's Bent, but gives sublime views west into Wales - Radnor, the Kerry Hills, Clun Forest - the Housman Welsh border country. This is also possibly the finest and yet least known view of Wenlock Edge, with the Long Mynd and Caer Caradoc beyond, and finally at the north of the dale, the Wrekin. Below, the Corve flows down to meet the Teme in the flood meadows under the ramparts of Ludlow Castle.

Loveliest of trees, the cherry now
Is hung with bloom along the bough,
And stands about the woodland ride
Wearing white for Eastertide.

Now, of my threescore years and ten,
Twenty will not come again,
And take from seventy springs a score,
It only leaves me fifty more.

And since to look at things in bloom
Fifty springs are little room,
About the woodlands I will go
To see the cherry hung with snow.

ASL II

The road that takes a very steep final descent from Hayton's Bent eventually leads to the valley bottom at Lower Hayton. But not before it has turned and twisted through one of the most rural and deep of these ancient lanes that wind hereabout. Past an old former cider house, the Hen and Chickens, with its huge six foot deep walls; a half-timbered farmhouse so typical of the dale called the Manor House; and past weather-boarded barns, a vernacular feature of Corvedale farm building. Sixty years ago, cider houses were far more common in this part of Corvedale than inns. Now lost on old over-grown bridle ways, a matching Hen and Ferret, not more than half a mile away from the Lower Hayton Hen and Chickens, slaked the thirst of those who regularly walked from here into Ludlow every day. Our older neighbours tell of Mrs Rudd, who lived in the cottage in which my husband and I now live, from the 1920s to the 1940s and who carried two large baskets full of produce into Ludlow every day of the week. This would have been an eighteen mile walk every day.

The former lack of wheeled transport (unavailable to the average tenant farmer) goes part way to explain why this particular area of Corvedale is criss-crossed by a series of deep green lanes - "ways" in the vernacular. They take more direct routes uphill and downdale and they still exist quite extensively on these slopes of the Corvedale. They are high-hedged and full of England's native trees - the sweet chestnut, the lime, the ash and the oak. Along these old green lanes, and still found in the woods hereabouts, wild cherry (prunus avium) casts its blossom - a wonderful sight.

There is still much old meadow land around with plenty of visual evidence of ridge and furrow. Much of this eastern hillside running along the Corve has fragments of ancient woodland. On clear, cold winter days, this run of ancient woodland from Stanton Lacy Wood, to Witchcot Wood and on to Sutton Hill Coppice is perhaps to be seen at its best. And frequently well defined in the winter sunshine with sharp shadows below these woods lie fields bearing the humps and furrows of old medieval ploughland. Banked up below the woods are large mounds, now grassed over, where the ancient ploughs turned and threw the soil into its resting place.

Once, only twenty years ago, these little fields were also spread yellow in spring with the beautiful wild double daffodil. Even more rare, there were meadows with the ravishing autumn crocus. Although we felt like despicable criminals at the time I must now honestly confess that I am glad my mother and I took some of these autumn crocus bulbs. We translated them over a few hedgerows and gave them new life in our own paddock. They still flourish within the confines of her protection. Those that we took them from have now perished under the herbicide sprayer.

The once common but now slightly rarer lady smocks are still with us and, increasing their stock and strength, oxslips are returning to the banks of these old green ways. It is the woods here though, which are still strongly resplendent in their beauty. A succession of spring flowers spreads across these ancient woodland floors; the wood anemone (the windflower), primroses, violets white and purple and bluebells in profusion. There are the subtle green blossoms of dog's mercury and herb Paris. In summer crab apple blossom follows and in autumn the trees themselves provide the year's final flourishing of colour - pineneedles, chestnuts of both varieties, beech nuts, rose hips, and little green and red crab apples.

In my own shire, if I was sad,

Homely comforters I had:

The earth, because my heart was sore,

Sorrowed for the son she bore;

And standing hills, long to remain,

Shared their short-lived comrade's pain.

And bound for the same bourn as I,

On every road I wandered by,

Trod beside me, close and dear,

The beautiful and death-struck year:

Whether in the woodland brown

I heard the beechnut rustle down,

And saw the purple crocus pale

Flower about the autumn dale;

Or littering far the fields of May

Lady-smocks a-bleaching lay,

And like a skylit water stood

The bluebells in the azured wood.

Yonder, lightening other loads,

The seasons range the country roads,

But here in London streets I ken

No such helpmates, only men;

And these are not in plight to bear,

If they would, another's care.

They have enough as 'tis:

I see in many an eye that measures me

The mortal sickness of a mind

Too unhappy to be kind.

Undone with misery, all they can

Is to hate their fellow man;

And till they drop they needs must still

Look at you and wish you ill.

ASL XLI

Back on the higher ground beyond Hayton's Bent lie a series of deserted medieval villages.
On reflection, it is easy to see why they became deserted during the great climate changes with took particular hold around 1315-1317. This ground lies high, most of it over 800 feet, and it is very exposed. The wind can blow cruelly across it. The names of these places bear witness to their exposure - Bitterley, Cold Weston. Records show that the summers of 1315 to 1317 were devastatingly wet and cold; crops were ruined and life on this high ground must have become unbearably hard. These bad summers were one of a series of events which culminated in the great scourge of the Black Death in 1349. We surmise, confidently I believe, that it must have been the succession of all these events which finally drove the survivors from these high, marginal settlements to seek a new life on the lower, more sheltered lands of the dales.

Coming from Ludlow and Hayton's Bent, the first of these deserted sites to be reached is Witchcot. Today all that remains is a series of hollows, mounds of green grass and associated earthworks. All were mentioned in Domesday. Witchcot in later centuries became encapsulated in one, large, magnificent farmhouse with walled farmyard - now found in ruins down a track from the top road not far from Hayton's Bent. Next comes Postons, (Possetone of Domesday) Lesser and Greater. The villagers of Postons were bound, 800 years ago, to supply Shrewsbury Abbey with box branches for the Palm Sunday service.

At Greater Poston the ground rises again. Lurkey Hill bends round towards Stoke St Milborough found via Scirmidge Lane and The Thrift. Our top road leads on to 'The Gorse', the local name for Cold Weston Hill, where sits little Cold Weston church with its Norman arched doorway, and a quarter of a mile off the road on a semi-circular site. Green lanes lead up and around, and the signs of the former medieval village lie in the earthworks of the surrounding fields. It is the saddest and loneliest of these little churches hereabouts, once a chapel belonging to the Manor of Morville (in the north of the county), and thence transferred to the protection of Shrewsbury Abbey.

The story of Cold Weston church is typical but sad. Over the 1960's and 1970's it had a diminishing, small but devoted parish community of six or eight regular worshippers. (Roughly a quarter of the total parish. Even in 1540 there were only two farmhouses here). Services were held once a month in summer. The farmer's wife at nearby Hollybush Farm baked the bread that was broken at the Eucharist. She and her husband polished the pews and lectern and carried flowers from their garden up the thousand year old track to the church. Its ancient yews guard the burial ground of the circular churchyard, pointing to a pre-Christian use. In 1980 the vicar, who served several of these tiny parishes, retired simultaneously with the farmers of Hollybush retiring into Ludlow. There are some poignant comments in the Cold Weston Parish Register by its last serving priest: "1975 - Lovely summer weather with just an unsettled period now and then - but falling congregations after being so good earlier in the year - very sad but I must go on"; for 1977 "A summer of changeable weather but one in which the Cold Weston summer had generally dry conditions" and then his last entry was made: "1980, 24th August. Douglas S M Lockhart ended his ministry in this ancient parish with the church on the hill. 1973-1980. DSML, Rector of Bitterley, Priest in Charge and Sequester."

As ever, some stalwarts fought to save this remote, beautiful little church and its graveyard.
Today it stands for sale from the Church Commissioners.

Hopton Cangeford, a former fine Georgian church, and formerly served by the same minister as Cold Weston (Douglas Lockhart cycled between the two) is some two miles to the south east of Cold Weston by bridle path. It, too, is no longer a serving, consecrated church. It once came complete with squire's pew, fireplace all hung round with fading red velvet curtains. It has now been converted to residential use.

From Cold Weston Hill the vision to westward is impressive, stretching across and over Corvedale to Wenlock Edge; beyond the Edge lies the long ridge of the Stretton Hills, and further west are ranged the undulating hills beyond the Clun valley and into Wales. To the east, the sweep of Brown Clee runs into the wonderful volcanic shape of Titterstone Clee, and beyond stand the Malverns and May Hill in Gloucestershire.

The lane from Cold Weston delves deeper into remote hilly countryside with even remoter hamlets and farmsteads, still clinging to their cherished names of Pel Beggar, Peckledy and Tana Leas. Here one attains a totally secluded area, very characteristic of the more obscure settlements of South Shropshire. It is almost a world within another world. The small village of Clee St Margaret, with its deep running ford flowing straight through the middle of the village, is the largest settlement before the lane turns to take its highest course to round Brown Clee to its other side. It is a rare vision of a secluded, working rural English village with its local sandstone houses, Saxon church with Norman herringbone stone work, sheltered cottage gardens and old orchards.

Not far away on these high folds of Brown Clee stands the exquisite Norman chapel of Heath, untroubled and quiet in a grassy field. Heath, too, is a site of a former deserted medieval village and the chapel is listed in Domesday as a berewick of Worthen, of the deanery of Pontesbury, north west of Corvedale. The Chapel is a lovely example of a Normal chapel and is over 850 years old. It never had any burial rights, but a medieval grave slab was found during restorations which took place in 1912. At that time, the architect Basil Stallybrass had been engaged by the locally eminent Powell family of Sutton Court, some three miles away from Heath, to design and oversee the construction of a music room for them. He had also been commissioned by the Society for the Protection of Ancient Buildings to visit Heath chapel where he at once saw that the building was in danger of collapsing. The buttresses were coming away from the walls and thus the walls were unsupported. A programme of restoration took place which saved the chapel from sure ruin and it was during the ensuing restoration that the medieval grave slab was found. This was put back in the chancel, probably its most likely original resting place.

There are no records of burials at all at the Heath. The dead were taken to Stoke St Milborough for internment. But there is often a wish to be buried near the ground one used to plough. In 1937 burial rights were granted to a little piece of ground near the old Chapel yard, but the earliest marked grave is 1959. However, one of the old green ways that crossed the hillside from Peckledy to Tugford crosses the lane at the corner of the Chapel yard and there was an old four-cross just through a field gate where the crossroads passed. Gone now, but the tops of two stones were once visible, and the site was always pointed out to a new tenant of Heath Farm because here was buried a suicide victim - just who had long been forgotten over sixty years ago. But a commentary that even here, with no traditional burial rights, the shunned were committed across the chapel yard hedge row into unconsecrated ground.

Sinner's Rue

I walked alone and thinking,
And faint the nightwind blew
And stirred on mounds at crossways
The flower of sinner's rue.

Where the roads part they bury
Him that his own hand slays,
And so the weed of sorrow
Springs at the four cross ways.

By night I plucked it hueless,
When morning broke 'twas blue:
Blue at my breast I fastened
The flower of sinner's rue.

It seemed a herb of healing,
A balsam and a sign,
Flower of a heart whose trouble
Must have been worse than mine.

Dead clay that did me kindness,
I can do none to you,
But only wear for breastknot
The flower of sinner's rue.

LP XXX

The ancient green ways here are even deeper than those a mile back at Cold Weston. The old lane which ran through the deserted village of Heath from Tugford is probably the one alluded to in a document which exists from 1612 about 'strakers' rights on Brown Clee. Strakers were those people who lived a few miles below the two twin peaks of Brown Clee called Abdon Burf and Clee Liberty and not actually right up on the hill itself. They were those who lived in and around such places as Heath or Tugford but who nevertheless had a free right to graze their cattle on Brown Clee.

The document is entitled 'A Description of the Clee Lordships, Commoners and Strakers adjoined made about 1612'. It lists 28 little townships on both sides of Brown Clee who had rights on the common. Strakers were expected to use the green ways to pass with their livestock up onto the high common ground of the hill. Today, as in 1612, the hill was jealously guarded by the old families of Duce and Heighway. The 1612 regulations for those coming across Duce or Heighway land were strict.

> *"And the strakers Inhabiting in the Townships of the Heath, Norncott and Tugford are and have used to drive up their cattle along a way between the said Waste Soile of St Margaret's Clee and the Waste Soile of Abdon, near unto a place called the Kings Shield, and there are to put of their cattle in the s'd place called the Hay Meadow being parcell of the said Clives alias Brown Clee as aforesaid, and if they Staff drive or put them off before they come to that place they have been used to be fined and amerced at the Swanimott Court[1]."*

The strakers of Heath and Tugford finally lost their rights of common pasture on Brown Clee with the Enclosure Acts of the 18th century, but freeholders of Clee St Margaret still preserved their rights up until 1976. They in turn guarded their rights as strictly as their forebears in 1612. Even in the early years of this century the non-freeholders would gain in boldness and send their livestock up on to the free pasture. Eventually the Duce and Heighway families would plan a raid on a night of the full moon. Horsemen galloped across the Clee blowing bugles and hunting horns and the like. The trespassers' animals were gathered up and rounded off the common. For devilment many were sent right down to the Corve valley villages of Tugford and Bouldon via Kidnall Gutter and there left for their owners to find. Such stories were readily told and repeated on winter nights at The Three Horseshoes Inn at Wheathill - a high point in the 'pass' between Titterstone Clee and Brown Clee - and down at the Tally Ho! in Bouldon, both still the nearest inns to these hamlets of the Clee.

Abdon Burf at 1,765ft today is the highest peak in Shropshire. Destroyed by quarrying for its basalt of *dhu* stone, the summit of Abdon Burf was once an Iron Age site of 40 circles of stone, enclosed within one large outer circle, or vallum. Geologists have recorded that this enclosed area measured 1,317ft from north to south and 660ft from east to west. (The quarrying no longer takes place on Brown Clee and hence the disparity in heights of former Shropshire reference books. Its height was genuinely reduced by the quarrying, a point not lost on Housman himself. In 1934 Housman noted in a letter to Houston Martin "Abdon Burf is the highest part of Brown Clee, which is the highest hill in Shropshire, but will soon cease to be so, as they are quarrying the top away ..."!)

[1] *The Swanimott Court (or Swainmote Courts) were established in 1217 to protect the King's hunting rights in the South Shropshire and Herefordshire forest areas from straying beasts.*

The Iron Age site must have been wonderful and conjecture might lead us to suppose that it was the site of both burial and worship. The medieval writer Leland records *"Cle Hills be holy in Shropshire"*. It would not be mere romantic fantasy to conclude that Abdon Burf and its twin peak Clee Liberty (on which also stood Iron Age remains which were also destroyed by quarrying) were almost certainly revered sites of the ancient hill worshippers. For those who climb the summits today the distant view will appear just as it did to those ancient people who were drawn to its heights thousands of years ago. Cader Idris, the Brecon Beacons and Radnor of Wales, the Malverns, the Cheshire Plain and the nearer Shropshire hills of the Wrekin, Long Mynd and Stiperstones stand framing the far horizons today as they have done for centuries.

Below, lying between the townships of Abdon and Clee St Margaret rises Nordy Bank, once believed to have been created as a Roman encampment but now confirmed as an earlier Iron Age fortress. Its huge earthbanks are massive and all-encompassing, today covered in bracken; in spring a verdant green, a deep russet brown in autumn and winter. It is a solitary and isolated site. Giving commanding views to the south, with its steep escarpment and difficult location, it must have provided a safe haven for the Celtic tribes who were the hill's early masters.

The tiny village of Abdon, mentioned in that 'Description of the Clee' is indeed an ancient site. Its church is not as architecturally interesting as that of Heath, but its setting certainly makes up for that. High on the most western flank of Brown Clee, below the highest point in Shropshire, Abdon Burf, the deserted medieval village is again seen as earthworks in the field adjoining the churchyard. A little wooden wicket gate leads into this field, and a deep ancient green way runs from the other side of the church, where a stile and old worn stones lead down hill to the little settlement of Abdon today.

Abdon is in many senses the pure evocation of a Shropshire settlement as described by Housman in his poems. It is very remote, it is set high, but sheltered in the fold of the hill. It faces west. A deep lane runs right through the farmyard where still the dog runs down the yard to greet the wayfarer. Each little house or farmstead has an orchard and the pear trees are old and stately. Their branches in the spring are arranged like wonderous candelabra, decked out in white, standing high over the hedge rows to shower their blossom.

Down from Abdon the land falls away into the Corve valley and rises up to form Wenlock Edge. On this side of Corvedale the land is of heavy red clay and hard to work for those who plough. As meadow land it is verdant, green and rich with clover. West from Abdon the hills blend into the Welsh border and the sunsets never fail to impress from this high vantage point. As if to match the excellence of the sunsets, the banks and hedgerows around Abdon abound in laburnum. In May, Abdon Burf is hung with golden chains of laburnum flowers in the hedgerows.

The churchyard is old and semi-circular with yew trees. Undoubtedly an old burial ground, there are stones to the Hughes and Rudd families who have worked and farmed these upland areas for many years. One cross of white stone has counterparts in many a foreign field. It commemorates a Shropshire lad who died in the Great War, one who will never grow old. Alongside there is Fanny and Dick. To see Abdon today is to see Shropshire through Housman's eyes back in 1896.

Fancy's Knell

When lads were home from labour
At Abdon under Clee,
A man would call his neighbour
And both would send for me.
And where the light in lances
Across the mead was laid,
There to the dances
I fetched my flute and played.

The youth toward his fancy
Would turn his brow of tan,
And Tom would pair with Nancy
And Dick step off with Fan;
The girl would lift her glances
To his, and both be mute:
Well went the dances
At evening to the flute.

Ours were idle pleasures,
Yet oh, content we were,
The young to wind the measures,
The old to heed the air;
And I to lift with playing
From tree and tower and steep
The light delaying,
And flute the sun to sleep.

Wenlock Edge was umbered,
And bright was Abdon Burf,
And warm between them slumbered
The smooth green miles of turf;
Until from grass and clover
The upshot beam would fade,
And England over
Advanced the lofty shade.

The lofty shade advances,

I fetch my flute and play:

Come, lads, and learn the dances

And praise the tune to-day.

To-morrow, more's the pity,

Away we both must hie,

To air the ditty,

And to earth I.

LP XLI

Chapter Three

Far in a Western Brookland
- The Corve Dale

Far in a western brookland

That bred me long ago

The poplars stand and tremble

By pools I used to know.

There, in the windless night-time,

The wanderer, marvelling why,

Halts on the bridge to hearken

How soft the poplars sigh.

He hears: no more remembered

In fields where I was known,

Here I lie down in London

And turn to rest alone.

There, by the starlit fences,

The wanderer halts and hears

My soul that lingers sighing

About the glimmering weirs.

ASL LII

Far in a Western Brookland
- The Corve Dale

The Corve is not a river that meanders. Its course is direct as it leaves the upper reaches of the dale in the north and then flows southwards between Wenlock Edge and Brown Clee towards Culmington, Stanton Lacy and then into the Teme at Ludlow. It is sped on its way by a series of tributary brooks which, like the Corve, can be swift and rapid in full spate.

The Corve and its brooks have a vast catchment area of the high ground of Brown Clee Hill and Wenlock Edge. There is Clee Brook, Strand Brook, Pye Brook and Trow Brook to name but a few and a host of dingles draining off the high lands.

The land of Corvedale is therefore a rewarding one to farm for those who work hard. On the east of the Corve's banks the soil is heavy, red clay. There have been good returns for those who have worked them over the centuries which goes a long way to explain why Corvedale is also rich in history. The dale was a busy medieval throughway with its Hundreds of Culmington and Munslow. The market towns of Ludlow and Much Wenlock at either end are still market towns today, but in the middle ages the wool trade hereabouts was good enough to support another market at Munslow (roughly mid-way along the dale). Those who farmed here 900 years ago were good with sheep, as their successors are today. Only recently has the local breed, the Clun, native to Shropshire, been superseded on a lot of Corvedale farms by Texels and Suffolks. Wool made Corvedale and Ludlow rich and prosperous for many centuries and has contributed largely to the wealth of medieval history in the dale.

Medieval Corvedale was established rapidly with the Norman conquest. A series of defensive castles and strongholds were stationed along the dale's length.

Of these Corvedale lands Domesday refers much to one Helgot, whence the local name of Holdgate; today a tiny settlement in the north of the dale. Helgot possessed many manors along the Corve, and a total of sixteen in the county as a whole. At the time of the Norman conquest Holdgate was known as Stanton, and an existing church with a serving priest and a castle are recorded there in Domesday. Helgot the Norman chose to establish his main headquarters at Stanton and he built a new castle, the remains of which can still clearly be seen. Helgot's castle is today part of a working farm (as it has been for centuries now). The front of the farm is deceptive; it looks just as a good Shropshire working farm should; but then to the rear one is almost transported back to medieval France. A high, solid and mighty round sandstone tower, that would not look out of place at Poitiers or Anjou, rises out of the farmhouse walls. At the first time of seeing it is most impressive, and in its unaltered simplicity, for me, is far more evocative than the grander castles of, say, Warwick or Leeds.

In the 12th century a new church was built within the perimeter of the castle. This was the early beginnings of Holdgate's church, The Holy Trinity.

The interior of the church at Holdgate is one of the most atmospheric in the dale. I last visited it late on a winter's afternoon. The sun was sinking low over the far hills, the old earthworks of the deserted village in the field opposite were heightened in the winter light. The sky was clear and cold and a wind was starting to get up. The Norman archway is impressive at any time, but inside the wind was rattling round the tower, the Saxon carvings around the font were caught in a last shaft of light. The pews are thought to date from the later middle ages and in the fading light figures of the past were easily conjured.

Outside the church is the motte and bailey raised by Helgot. It is now covered in little wild daffodils in the spring and, like the church, radiates a deep feeling of the antiquity of the site.

The daffodils of Helgot's fortifications are preceded nearby with drifts of snowdrops which flower along the banks of the Strand Brook and all the hedgerows of the lanes between Tugford and Bouldon are white with the flowers when winter's first defences are down and the flowers peep through. They are a wonderful presence and it is a joy to make the annual winter pilgrimage to see them again pin their abundant masses. Later will come violets and primroses.

The Lent Lily

'Tis spring; come out to ramble
The hilly brakes around,
For under thorn and bramble
About the hollow ground
The primroses are found.

And there's the windflower chilly
With all the winds at play,
And there's the Lenten lily
That has not long to stay
And dies on Easter day.

And since till girls go maying
You find the primrose still,
And find the windflower playing
With every wind at will,
But not the daffodil,

Bring baskets now, and sally
Upon the spring's array,
And bear from hill and valley
The daffodil away
That dies on Easter day.

ASL XXIX

Tugford and Bouldon are typical tiny settlements along the Corve valley. Both are ancient sites and Tugford, like Holdgate, has a pretty church with Norman detailing. Bouldon lies tucked away in the folds of the hillside where the Clee Brook runs down to where it once drove Bouldon mill. There were obviously stonemasons in Bouldon, for examples of their work can be found on the 18th century tombstones in the Cold Weston churchyard. Other anonymous earlier stonemasons were responsible for the wonderful fertility figures - sheila-na-gigs - adorning Tugford's church. They are a little local Corvedale curiosity with similar fulsome ladies at Diddlebury and back at Holdgate. They also appear over the hills at Church Stretton.

As the medieval highway wanders on from Holdgate towards Tugford, the tower of Broncroft Castle rises out of the trees. It is a fine edifice built of the local sandstone which glows a warm honey colour in the orange evening sunlight. Broncroft is the only castle in Corvedale to remain standing and has continued to remain inhabited through the centuries to this day. In the romantic revival of the Pre-Raphaelite's desire to recreate gothic medievalism, Broncroft proved a wonderful starting point and was given some fine additions. Much of Broncroft's oldest 14th century building is still intact and its builder in 1345 was Sir John Burley.

Burley was a tutor to Richard II and fought alongside the Black Prince. He and his brother Simon Burley were two of the original Knights of the Garter. One hundred years later their descendant Joan Burley married into the Lyttleton family. At the time of the Civil War, Broncroft had fallen into a Worcestershire family's protection. They were the Barneby's who held Broncroft until 1645 when the Parliamentarians seized it as a prison for Royalist captives.

After the war, Broncroft Castle was mentioned in a special Act of Parliament of 1648 declaring that the castle be made 'untenable'. This really prevented the castle from ever being a defensive building again, and the architectural consequence of the Act was the reduction in the height of the two towers, thus rendering Broncroft unable to sustain any further fortified campaign. The towers were reinstated in 1830, followed by other 19th century refurbishments. A later owner, Dr Francis Pember, left a final memorial to all past occupiers of the castle in a set of stained glass windows which bear the coats of arms of all the families who have lived at Broncroft. These arms remain a splendid feature in the windows of the 31ft drawing room of today.

A little distance from Broncroft, continuing along the old medieval highway, is the small settlement of Peaton, standing on the Pye Brook, and near to the banks of the Corve. Here lies the last of Corvedale's three castles, Corfham. Its remains lie on the meadows between the Pye Brook and the River Corve itself. The site is guarded and enfolded in the dale by Wenlock Edge and its nearer hillside rising to the high ground of Brown Clee Hill; to the south the valley's final miles stretch to Ludlow flanked by Mortimer's Forest and Bringwood Chase rising beyond. Of all the Corvedale strongholds, Corfham more than any other became entangled with the mighty power brokers of the middle ages. Today, only the tell-tale clumps of rank nettles mingled with the quite substantial earthworks are the loan guardians of its former secrets.

Walking today over the grassy meadows on which Corfham Castle stood and observing the many earthworks around, it is easy to imagine that this must once have been a sizeable stronghold. The old 12th century Manor of Corfham included the Corvedale settlements of Diddlebury, Siefton

and Culmington, and the Victorian Shropshire historian John Corbet Anderson quotes *"here was a gallows, assize of bread and beer, and held pleas of bloodshed, hue and cry, with other lesser pleas"*. Corfham's place in history was at its height during the Plantagenets' reign. In the 1170's Corfham was held by Walter de Clifford. Clifford, together with the Clares and FitzAlans, was one of the great Marcher families, who under the leadership of Henry II, were suppressing the Welsh lands over the border. These families were creating a formidable system of defence and administration in the area and fashioning a powerful and esteemed Marcher society. It is a mix which has largely lasted through to this century - a blend of Saxon and Celt; Norman mixed with Welsh.

The main protagonist in Corfham's past was the mighty Henry II, the Plantagenet King, married to his equally formidable, powerful landed French Queen, Eleanor of Acquitaine. Here on the Corve water meadows, Henry met and fell in love with Clifford's daughter, Rosamund, whose beauty by all contemporary accounts was exquisite. The story of Fair Rosamund and Henry has passed into English folklore, and become embellished with stories of Eleanor's jealousy; of how the Queen offered Rosamund a choice of death by either a poisoned chalice or dagger. Locally, however, Rosamund's memory has continually been recorded over the centuries by the naming of a well near to the site of Corfham Castle; detailed Ordnance Survey maps still record and name Rosamund's Well on the left bank of the Corve, just a field away from the Castle's remains.

At Michaelmas 1178, Henry II gave Corfham Castle to Rosamund's father. Interestingly, however, in concealment of the reason for his generous gift to the father of his mistress, the new owner of Corfham remained anonymous on the Pipe Rolls until 1190.

As their relationship developed, Henry installed his lover at Woodstock Palace where she died. Was she poisoned at Eleanor's instigation? Rosamund Clifford was buried at Godstow Church and after Henry's death in 1189 her body was ignominiously exhumed and reburied beyond the churchyard walls.

The family rows which engulfed the Plantagenet off-spring of Eleanor and Henry then fell to haunt the de Clifford family and the future heirs of Corfham. When Rosamund's father died, Richard the Lionheart (Henry II's eldest son) had acceded to the throne and refused to allow the eldest Clifford son to inherit the Barony of Corfham. And so it passed to the second Clifford son, Richard de Clifford. During King Richard's famous absences at the crusades, the younger Plantagenet son John took the opportunity to restore Corfham to the elder Clifford brother, Walter. The manor of Corfham flourished throughout the 13th century and during the 14th century there were still titled Lords of Corfham. But by the 1320's the old Manor of Corfham had already gone. Today, the remains of Corfam Castle lie in grassy meadow land, where the cattle and sheep of Peaton Hall graze quietly on. But come rain or shine, year after year, the troubles of those who lived here and made our history are remembered only by the eternally thriving nettle, and its piercing sting. The former Plantagent stronghold walls have crumbled into the clay. Now, only the rank nettle weed marks the passage of kings.

With seed the sowers scatter

The furrows as they go;

Poor lads, 'tis little matter

How many sorts they sow,

For only one will grow.

The charlock on the fallow

Will take the traveller's eyes,

And gild the ploughland sallow

With flowers before it dies,

But twice 'twill not arise.

The stinging nettle only

Will still be found to stand:

The numberless, the lonely,

The thronger of the land,

The leaf that hurts the hand.

That thrives, come sun, come showers;

Blow east, blow west, it springs;

It peoples towns, and towers

About the court of Kings,

And touch it and it stings.

MP XXXII

Occasionally, relics of the past turn up quite literally. A gargoyle's head lies nonchalantly in the doorway of Peaton Hall. The tenant of the Hall farms the land on which Corfham Castle stands and found it amongst the earthworks. Tales at the Tally Ho! Inn at nearby Bouldon told of the pit at Peaton where bodies from an ancient skirmish had been buried. All considered as fanciful stuff laced with strong ale and cider until chance excavations at Fanny and Billy Brayne's sand pit at Bank Top, Peaton, revealed skeletons and armoury dating back to the 11th century.

Life along the Corvedale has stayed very much as it ever was across the centuries. Only in the last thirty years has the motor car and vastly improved agricultural equipment changed the way of life of the Dale.

The Tally Ho! was one of only two inns along the old medieval highway. The other was the New Inn, and sited much nearer to Stanton Lacy and Ludlow. The Tally Ho! served almost half the Corvedale community and as such was far more than a pub. Tucked below Bouldon Bank with the Clee Brook passing its little garden it was once a main-stay of social life in the area. Its red quarry tiled floor was worn down with boots that had walked miles across fields and streams to reach it; the benches were arranged around three of its walls and the tables had two centuries of beer and cider staining their tops, and the dominos sticky with yet more of the same. The walls were thick yellow with smoke and it was a brave person from outside the dale that every opened the door to walk in! Many of Housman's lads, now grown old, used the Tally Ho! as their surrogate home. Between five and six of an evening many would come in from their hedge pleaching, their fence mending or their scything and have tea.

Like an old hiring fair, the customers of the Tally Ho! could be identified by their tools of work propped up against the fence outside. Tea came from a tin of sardines, some buttered bread, the latter was delivered down the dale from Prices bakery in Ludlow and was usually washed down with some cider. For the Tally Ho! at Bouldon was far more than an inn. It also sold bacon, tea, cheese and washing powder amongst other products. During my childhood it was called The Omo Pub in celebration of the brand of washing powder it sold. If the rain streamed from stone and hillock too violently, or snow swept down Bouldon Bank against the window panes, then some of those arranged on the benches inside would just stay there all night until the tempest ceased. The Ludlow Hunt are still meeting outside, and the locals within!

The distances between the more traditional type of two inns of this lower road in Corvedale was partly aided by an in-filling of cider houses along the way. Each little cottage had its own orchard, filled with cider apples, an abundance of Shropshire damsons, a pear tree and other apples. Each hamlet would help with the cider making and stone presses are still to be found at some of the cottages here. A lot of these orchards have still survived, monuments to a self-sufficiency that was absolutely essential. Even in the 1950's and early 1960's, most smallholders only had one smoky diesel tractor. I count myself privileged to have witnessed hay making by scythe in Corvedale, and whilst we raked the hay and tossed it loosely into Dutch barns I was told of how on moonlight nights, lamps were hung on staves to light the meadows and the stone cider flagons helped the gentle rhythm of scything to pass more sweetly and easily as the hours passed.

The chestnut casts his flambeaux, and the flowers
Stream from the hawthorn on the wind away,
The doors clap to, the pane is blind with showers.
Pass me the can, lad, there's an end of May.

There's one spoilt spring to scant our mortal lot,
One season ruined of our little store.
May will be fine next year as like as not:
Oh ay, but then we shall be twenty-four.

We for a certainty are not the first
Have sat in taverns while the tempest hurled
Their hopeful plans to emptiness, and cursed
Whatever brute and blackguard made the world.

It is in truth iniquity on high
To cheat our sentenced souls of aught they crave,
And mar the merriment as you and I
Fare on our long fool's-errand to the grave.

Iniquity it is; but pass the can.

My lad, no pair of kings our mother bore;

Our only portion is the estate of man:

We want the moon, but we shall get no more.

If here to-day the cloud of thunder lours

To-morrow it will hie on far behests;

The flesh will grieve on other bones than ours

Soon, and the soul will mourn in other breasts.

The troubles of our proud and angry dust

Are from eternity, and shall not fail.

Bear them we can, and if we can we must.

Shoulder the sky, my lad, and drink your ale.

LP IX

Communities amongst these little townships were very dependent upon each other for help. A main annual event was the salting of the pig. Each cottage had a pig sty and even today the paint on the wall in our pantry flakes off on the wall against which the salted pig was hung. Neighbours helped each other in this ritual slaughter of an animal whose meat would help them through a long winter. Ludlow was a long way in drifting snow, driving rain and Corvedale's clinging, red, heavy mud.

This area is still as feudal in its system of land ownership with lord and tenant as it was in the middle ages. Now there are not quite so many barons and lords of the manor. However, much of Corvedale even today is split between two major titled landowners - The Earl of Plymouth of Oakly Park at the south of the dale and Viscount Boyne of Burwarton on the far side of Brown Clee who retains land in the middle of the dale around Peaton. But the tenants' year is as recognisable as it was in those past ages. Rent is due on Lady Day; tenancies run from Michaelmas or St John's Day (midsummer's day) and shooting rights are jealously guarded. At Downton Hall at Whitbach, in the south of the dale, the last and direct descendants of Lord Ismay, owner of the fated SS Titanic, lived Lady Rouse Boughton and her daughter Lady Mary. Lady Rouse Boughton and her daughter were Joint Masters of Ludlow Hunt. Before she died in 1975 Lady Rouse Boughton continued to ride side saddle. Adorned in black, with her hat and veil, she took every hedge and fence as they came and was thus respected for her riding by the local earth-stoppers. Each year, the earth-stoppers, estate workers and tenants were invited to Downton Hall and a scene not dissimilar from Hardy's vision of Bathsheba Everdene at the harvest home supper, with Gabriel Oak and the assembled company, would unfold. Tables, as described by Hardy, would reach out from the windows arranged with a grand spread. A clay pigeon tournament was held with a prize for the ablest shooter. Of course, the custom ended with her death.

Both Lady Rouse Boughton and her daughter Lady Mary are buried in the tiny churchyard at Middleton, a couple of miles from their home. Middleton church, as so many in this area, is of Norman origin. It is tucked far away from the roaming of modern man and easy to miss for those who seek it out in its quietness. For those who do find it, it is a little treasure with a fine Elizabethan pulpit.

Back across the dale under the Wenlock Edge escarpment lies the village of Diddlebury. A wonderful view of virtually the whole expanse of the Corvedale can be gained from Diddlebury's churchyard. It is easier to make out the little smallholdings with their cider orchards on the opposite bank from here. They stretch in succession towards Ludlow with their evocative names of Lydehole, Titterhill and The Hopes. Equally, many of those who have lived and worked in the dale finally come to rest here in this churchyard. Many only ever left England to fight in the King's Shropshire Light Infantry during the Great War and then travelled no further than Knighton with their sheep again. These people have been the true fashioners of Corvedale's history.

The winds out of the west land blow,
My friends have breathed them there;
Warm with the blood of lads I know
Comes east the sighing air.

It fanned their temples, filled their lungs,
Scattered their forelocks free;
My friends made words of it with tongues
That talk no more to me.

Their voices, dying as they fly,
Loose on the wind are sown;
The names of men blow soundless by,
My fellows' and my own.

Oh lads, at home I heard you plain,
But here your speech is still,
And down the sighing wind in vain
You hollo from the hill.

The wind and I, we both were there,
But neither long abode;
Now through the friendless world we fare
And sigh upon the road.

ASL XXXVIII

Chapter Four

On Wenlock Edge

On Wenlock Edge the wood's in trouble;

His forest fleece the Wrekin heaves;

The gale, it plies the saplings double,

And thick on Severn snow the leaves.

'Twould blow like this through holt and hanger

When Uricon the city stood:

'Tis the old wind in the old anger,

But then it threshed another wood.

Then, 'twas before my time, the Roman

At yonder heaving hill would stare:

The blood that warms an English yeoman,

The thoughts that hurt him, they were there.

There, like the wind through woods in riot,

Through him the gale of life blew high;

The tree of man was never quiet:

Then 'twas the Roman, now 'tis I.

The gale, it plies the saplings double,

It blows so hard, 'twill soon be gone:

To-day the Roman and his trouble

Are ashes under Uricon.

ASL XXXI

On Wenlock Edge - Wenlock Edge, Ape Dale & Hope Dale

Border lands have always been fought over. Housman's corner of South Shropshire is Marches country and it is Wenlock Edge, a sharp escarpment of some ten to twelve miles in length, running north-south down Corvedale, which separates the English parts of South Shropshire from its upland Welsh border hill country.

Of all Housman's poems, it is perhaps On Wenlock Edge that gives a timeless sense of continuity between the Roman foot soldier who struggled here so long ago and the later wars that followed on this same land over the centuries. The Roman struggled with the border land in his time, then followed Owen Glendower, The Black Prince and the Wars of the Roses. Again in the later era of the Civil War, this area was fiercely contested by the King's followers and the Parliamentarians who pursued them here to fight. It is a salutary lesson that life is transitory - but Wenlock Edge (one of the oldest geological sites in the world) - remains to shoulder the burden of the passing real and metaphysical storms.

No fanciful vision either was Housman's Roman of the poem. The Roman and his trouble were very much here two thousand years ago. Somewhere near here Caractacus was captured by the occupying Roman forces and taken to Rome. Was it the Iron Age fort on the dramatic summit of Caer Caradoc, (meaning Hill of Caractacus) with its massive fortified ditches on steep heights, rising between Wenlock Edge and the Long Mynd, from which Caractacus was torn? Scholars are divided in their view of where this great battle, lead by our great British warrior ancestor, did actually take place. Tacitus, the Roman scholar, describes a wild hillside, steep, and with fortifications on its summit and a river below. This certainly fits the topography of Caer Caradoc near Wenlock Edge. We do know that Caractacus and his tribe, the Ordovices, were here in this border area being pushed by the Romans into Celtic Welsh territory. And we know that today's A49, running underneath Caer Caradoc, was once a Roman highway.

Wenlock Edge stands between the two Roman towns of Bravonium and Uriconium, the Leintwardine and Wroxeter of today respectively. A Roman milestone has weathered the centuries at Moston Pool, not far from Caradoc and the Edge, and there were major Roman encampments at Bromfield, just outside Ludlow and Stretford Bridge, a few miles south of Caer Caradoc. A main Roman highway, which linked the Severn estuary to Chester, ran parallel to the Edge between it and the Long Mynd.

Today, the memories of the Roman on Wenlock Edge are commemorated in a cluster of cottages on the western escarpment called Roman Bank.

But of Housman's wood, much is left. The Edge is clothed with ancient woodland all along its northern face. It is rich with flora, and the woodland floor is a succession of beauty from spring to autumn. Along with the plentiful Shropshire spring flowers of primroses, violets - blue and white - wood anemones, bluebells, foxgloves, the rarer spurge laurel and spotted orchids find refuge in some of its remoter dells. The wood climbs to the top of the Edge, standing along the skyline, sometimes spilling over and down the dingles of the Corvedale side. To the north the Wrekin stands alone, between them at Buildwas flows the Severn, the division of east and west, England and Wales, Saxon and Celt.

The Welsh Marches

High the vanes of Shrewsbury gleam
Islanded in Severn stream;
The bridges from the steepled crest
Cross the water east and west.

The flag of morn in conqueror's state
Enters at the English gate:
The vanquished eve, as night prevails,
Bleeds upon the road to Wales.

Ages since the vanquished bled
Round my mother's marriage-bed;
There the ravens feasted far
About the open house of war:

When Severn down to Buildwas ran
Coloured with the death of man,
Couched upon her brother's grave
The Saxon got me on the slave.

The sound of fight is silent long
That began the ancient wrong;
Long the voice of tears is still
That wept of old the endless ill.

In my heart it has not died,
The war that sleeps on Severn side;
They cease not fighting, east and west,
On the marches of my breast.

Here the truceless armies yet
Trample, rolled in blood and sweat;
They kill and kill and never die;
And I think that each is I.

None will part us, none undo
The knot that makes one flesh of two,
Sick with hatred, sick with pain,
Strangling - When shall we be slain?

When shall I be dead and rid
Of the wrong my father did?
How long, how long, till spade and hearse
Put to sleep my mother's curse?

ASL XXVIII

Many who come to Wenlock Edge for the first time are surprised to find that the Edge is not a fine viewing place along the entire length of its ridge as might be supposed. It is because of the famous wood of the poem, which, when in leaf, does much to obscure the very fine view that might otherwise have been had. The wood reaches up on the northern escarpment right to the top of the Edge in many places, and for half of the year the extensive surrounding lands are hidden by greenery. Winter is therefore the best season to walk along the ridge, when the visions all around are truly impressive. It is no Striding Edge of Lake District proportions, but it does form a natural barrier between the richer agricultural lands of south Shropshire - the orchards, tiny homesteads hidden in wooded dingles, secluded hollows and farm lands of Corvedale and Ludlow - and the rocky, heather strewn uplands to the west of Clun, the Long Mynd, the Stiperstones and the final stretches of England's Shropshire border with Wales.

There are some impressive viewing points though, at the northern end, nearer Much Wenlock. Bare rocky cliffs descend steeply and precipitously giving uninterrupted extensive views across Ape Dale (the other side of the Edge to Corvedale) into the Welsh border.

It was on this exposed rocky promontory that Housman stood in the winter of 1895. It would be reasonable to surmise that he left the train at Presthope station, just below this section of the Edge, and walked up to the top. Some months later, in October 1896, he wrote to his brother Laurence: "I ascertained by looking down from Wenlock Edge that Hughley Church could not have much of a steeple. But as I had already composed the poem and could not invent another name that sounded so nice, I could only deplore that the church at Hughley should follow the bad example of the church at Brou, which persists in standing on a plain after Matthew Arnold has said that it stands among mountains. I thought of putting a note to say that Hughley was only a name, but then I thought that would merely disturb the reader. I did not apprehend that the faithful would be making pilgrimages to these holy places".

Hughley Church

Hughley Steeple

The vane on Hughley steeple
Veers bright, a far-known sign,
And there lie Hughley people,
And there lie friends of mine.
Tall in their midst the tower
Divides the shade and sun,
And the clock strikes the hour
And tells the time to none.

To south the headstones cluster,
The sunny mounds lie thick;
The dead are more in muster
At Hughley than the quick.
North, for a soon-told number,
Chill graves the sexton delves,
And steeple-shadowed slumber
The slayers of themselves.

To north, to south, lie parted,
With Hughley tower above,
The kind, the single-hearted,
The lads I used to love.
And, south or north 'tis only
A choice of friends one knows,
And I shall ne'er be lonely
Asleep with these or those.

ASL LXI

Actually, the self-criticism over the steeple at Hughley was not really warranted. St John the Baptist at Hughley is a fine 13th century small village church, with a beautifully proportioned clock tower and a wonderful weather vane. Ironically, there had been a steeple before it was demolished and in 1701 replaced with the square clock tower which stands today. Inside is one of the few remaining rood screens in Shropshire, and arguably the finest in the county. And, alas, the dead are still more in number at Hughley than the quick.

The railway which carried Housman from Bridgnorth via Ironbridge and Much Wenlock and then across Wenlock Edge was only closed in 1962. A tunnel took the track through the rocks at Presthope, through to the opposite side of the Edge with stations at Rushbury and Longville. These are tiny hamlets which nestle under the northwest escarpment.

Of the villages on this side of the Edge, Rushbury is by far the most beautiful. There are fine half-timbered houses, and the church of St Peter dates from around 1200 with familiar Norman herringbone masonry. There is a charming school and almshouses of the early 19th century. Their inscription reads thus:

> This School and almshouses
> were built and endowed by Benjamin
> the seventh son of the late
> Richard and Mary Wainwright
> of Stanway in the year 1821

Domesday records that a hawk's eerie existed at Rushbury and that there was a wood fit for fattening eleven swine. Rushbury, though, eventually suffered as many villages did during the appalling weather of the mid-14th century and in 1341 it was recorded: "destruction of wheat by tempest, murrain of sheep, poverty and desertion of tenants." Many centuries later, the railway brought a brief flush of life through Rushbury again. It was a popular spot for those who knew of its charms to alight and walk up Roman Bank to the top of the Edge. Now the railway, like the Roman and medievals many centuries before, has deserted Rushbury again.

The railway was a critical facility for the quarrying that took place at the northern end of the edge. The rocks of Wenlock Edge are ancient. The rocks quarried here are known as Wenlock Limestone and were deposited approximately 420 million years ago. Simple shallow quarrying has probably taken place for many centuries, but at Knowle Quarry, now owned by the National Trust, it is possible to walk round the quarry, which ceased to operate in the 1920's, and see kilns dating back to 1750.

The Corvedale side of the Edge is rich in remote ancient manor houses. Their simple, direct vernacular architecture remained unspoilt as time and wealth simply passed them by unaltered. The houses, lonely and isolated, have their store of local folklore and stories.

The most famous of all stories from Wenlock Edge, now firmly written into Shropshire legend, but seemingly historically correct, is of Major Smallman and Wilderhope Manor House. Smallman was an officer of the Royalist army and had returned one night to remote Wilderhope, his family home, to discover that the manor had been looted by Cromwellian troops. He gave pursuit, finding the Parliamentarians the other side of Wenlock Edge. After a successful ambush he began to make his way back to Wilderhope with some of his recovered possessions. However, another larger group of Cromwell's men swiftly followed him and Smallman reached Wilderhope where he hid until his pursuers gained the Manor.

The Manor is almost built into the side of the hillside, and by descending a chute (still to be seen) and jumping out onto the bank behind the house, Smallman fled on his horse. Back up the steep ridge behind Lutwyche he rode, where the trees are perpetually bent double from the strength of the prevailing, harsh wind and onto the Edge itself. The troops followed and were nearly upon the Major when he forced his horse to jump over the Edge at its steepest point. The horse perished, but Smallman flung himself into a crab apple growing between the limestone outcrops. His pursuers left him as dead. But he survived. Today the point is still marked on Ordnance Survey maps as Major's Leap.

Wilderhope Manor stands hidden away, off roads, in all its untouched 16th century simplicity; not a complicated late Tudor manor house, but a practical one built in the local stone. The manor was built by Major Smallman's ancestors, Francis and Edith Smallman, whose initials are recorded in the moulded plasterwork ceilings. A fine oak staircase winds the entire height of the house, ending its journey at the attic under a conical roof which takes the form of a tiled turret outside.

The house stands alone, entirely remote in the most ravishing of all imaginable wild settings. It faces south-east, on the hillside below the Edge almost imperceptible at first as the weathered stone blends with surrounding nature so perfectly. Trees on the windswept ridge above are twisted. Woods line the streams that fall down into Corvedale. Green meadows role downwards from the very front door. This a supremely simple, yet impressive house, which this corner of Shropshire is so lucky to have. Quiet, secluded, yet the wind blows fiercely; a house that changes with the seasons as they embrace it and the hillside on which it stands.

Wilderhope Manor

The Corvedale valley with ancient wooded hillsides, orchards and farms.

The poplars stand and tremble beside the waters of the River Corve.

Deserted lanes in Corvedale.
"Night welled through lane and hollow
And hushed the countryside."

Broncroft Castle. A private residence today that has been inhabited for over seven centuries.

The smooth green miles of Corvedale's rich turf, with Wenlock Edge rising beyond it.

"And like a skylit water stood
The bluebells in the azured wood".

The Japanese Housman cherry blossoms under Ludlow tower -
two of the poet's most enduring symbols united in spring sunshine.

Ludlow's Cattle Market, 1993, on its former site in Corve Street as it was in Housman's lifetime,
but still always held on a Monday.

Ludlow Cattle Market -
'There's chaps from the town and the field and the till and the cart'.

Tell me not here, it needs not saying,
   What tune the enchantress plays
In aftermaths of soft September
   Or under blanching mays,
For she and I were long acquainted
   And I knew all her ways.

On russet floors, by waters idle,
   The pine lets fall its cone;
The cuckoo shouts all day at nothing
   In leafy dells alone;
And traveller's joy beguiles in autumn
   Hearts that have lost their own.

On acres of the seeded grasses
   The changing burnish heaves;
Or marshalled under moons of harvest
   Stand still all night the sheaves;
Or beeches strip in storms for winter
   And stain the wind with leaves.

Possess, as I possessed a season,
   The countries I resign,
Where over elmy plains the highway
   Would mount the hills and shine,
And full of shade the pillared forest
   Would murmur and be mine.

For nature, heartless, witless nature,
   Will neither care nor know
What stranger's feet may find the meadow
   And trespass there and go,
Nor ask amid the dews of morning
   If they are mine or no.

LPXL

There are other fine houses near to Wilderhope, notably Shipton Hall which dates from 1587 and is built of the same limestone. It still has its late Tudor facade and has not been altered much internally since the 1750's. Both Shipton Hall and Lutwyche Hall, also built in 1587, were established on old settlement sites which formed a route across to the old market town of Much Wenlock.

Much Wenlock was never the stronghold that Ludlow was, nor played such a vital role in history. Much Wenlock owes its being to its religious foundations. Its well known ruined abbey of today came about through St Milburga, a Mercian princess who also gave her name to Stoke St Milborough on Brown Clee. She built a small convent at Wenlock around 680. She was a popular local saint and many legends about her obviously persisted. Her brothers had given her land around Brown Clee, hence today's village of Stoke St Milborough. Whilst she was on a visit there, a hostile suitor pursued her. She crossed the Corve to get back to the safety of Wenlock, and immediately she had reached the opposite banks the river violently rose in tumult and prevented her pursuer from crossing and following her.

Her convent was sacked in a raid by the Danes around 874 and such was her folklore popularity that a refoundation of her settlement took place about 1050. Not long after 1066 the Earl Roger de Montgomery made the church into an abbey. The town then grew up very much under the auspices of the Abbey. On 26 May 1101 St Milburga's remains were discovered (fortuitously?) by the monks who translated her in grand ceremony to her final resting place in front of the high altar of their new church. Miraculous cures continued to abound and were reported locally with much enthusiasm. This did much to continue the popularity of Much Wenlock as a local pilgrimage centre. Finally, during the Reformation, Wenlock Abbey was dissolved in 1539, but this rather overtly pretty market town persisted and has survived very charmingly into the 20th century.

The Guildhall, Much Wenlock

'Tis time, I think, by Wenlock town
The golden broom should blow;
The hawthorn sprinkled up and down
Should charge the land with snow.

Spring will not wait the loiterer's time
Who keeps so long away;
So others wear the broom and climb
The hedgerows heaped with may.

Oh tarnish late on Wenlock Edge,
Gold that I never see;
Lie long, high snowdrifts in the hedge
That will not shower on me.

ASL XXXIX

While the north-west side of Wenlock Edge is a fairly steep escarpment, its south-easterly opposite side is a mixture of dingles and secluded hollows and mid-way along its length lies little Hope Dale.

Hope Dale is utterly hidden high up in the folds of the Edge. It is a magical, far-away little place where there is more grass growing on its exceptionally narrow, high-hedged lanes than stones or asphalt. Indeed the Shropshire usage of the word 'hope' means a secluded hollow. There are only one or two scattered farms which have the privilege to farm here. It is to their credit that this small dale has retained its unique atmosphere. Many centuries ago the wood on the Edge must have been slowly cleared here to provide today's upland sheltered grass pastures.

The woods that cover the Edge once formed part of one of Shropshire's ancient forests. This was the Long Forest. At Upper Millichope there remains one of the oldest domestic (both in use and in scale) dwellings in the country. This was the house of the 'verderer'; the important position given in Norman times to a person who looked after this section of the Crown's forest and its game and coppicing. It is a noble dwelling, with classic Norman arched doorway, of simple rectangular shape with interesting early windows. A wonderful stone staircase leads up in the massive thickness of the walls. It also bears considerable signs of its capability to withstand attack.

I have often found, in these ancient stretches of woodland in Corvedale, patches of a richer, black, friable soil. Further delving has lead me to find traces of charcoal as past evidence of the charcoal burning that was carried out in these forests. In these secluded areas, with wooded hillsides followed by areas of open, exposed land where the wind continually batters against ancient hedgerows and rattles through roof rafters, it is easy to imagine why so many local stories are flavoured with spirits and shadows of the past, and folk heroes of Wenlock Edge have persisted to the present day.

Not far from Presthope, right up on the Edge, is the Ridgeway. Down below the Edge in the rocks is a cave. This place today is still known and marked by the Ordnance Survey as Ippikin's Rock. Ippikin was a locally celebrated bandit and robber. He used a cave there to store his stolen treasure and to hold conference with his cohorts. Ippikin and his gang were thus assembled in the cave one night when a violent thunderstorm struck. The lightening shattered the rocks above the cave; they tumbled down and blocked the entrance to the cave. So Ippikin, his band of robbers and their hoard of treasure were sealed in for ever more. It is said that those who venture to climb down and call out "Old Ippikin! Old Ippikin!" before the cave will be met by the form of the robber, slashing out wildly with chains.

Two miles from Ippikin's Rock is the little village of Easthope. There was a 13th century church, St Peter's, which was badly burnt in a fire in June 1928. Destroyed in the fire was a wonderful hour glass which had been fixed to the pulpit and by which the lengths of the sermons were regulated! Also destroyed was the original door with its sanctuary ring. Murderers could gain access and sanctuary by ringing upon the bell. (My old friends who used to tell me these stories were most particular to emphasise that it was always murderers who sought sanctuary here!) In June 1333 the priest, Will Garmston, killed John de Esthope, the church's patron. Many a sighting of Will Garmston has been reported over the centuries, perhaps by those trying the ale between Presthope and Easthope.

Not to be outdone, the farm near St Peter's also has a reported resident ghost. The farm was once connected with Wenlock Abbey and used as a cell by some monks. Two monks apparently quarrelled with each other and on the last final, violent occasion, they killed each other. They are buried in this fateful churchyard of St Peter's, near the yew. Their ghosts have never been seen, but the sounds of their fight to the death are said to echo between the graves at night time.

And then there is the place called Glattering Glat, still remembered and pointed out by locals. (Glat is used in the local vocabulary to mean a hole). The tale which they still tell is of a man who worked this land. He was murdered by his son, and in order to remove the body from the scene of the crime with some urgency, the son dragged his father's body right through the nearest hedge. The hedge has, since that day, obstinately refused to obey any attempt to repair it. Sheep apparently still wander through the breach.

Once off the only section of main road that runs across the Edge and down towards Church Stretton, it is easy to see - and feel - why these stories and superstitions live on in folk memory. The local people did not move great distances, stories were easily passed from one generation to another. The area too can be at one moment open and exposed to the violent elements, with visions of the dark clouds gathering over the Welsh hills and soon to be upon you, then at another turn it can be secluded, quiet, hemmed in with trees where sounds and shadows become twisted and exaggerated. At the end of summer, a swiftly travelling thunderstorm often strides across Wenlock Edge, the lightening still striking Ippikin's Rock as it did years ago. Across the valley from the Rock at Church Stretton they still remember their former 1st November fair day as Dead Man's Fair. The leaves from the wood blow down into the valleys on either side and the storm gathers again on Wenlock Edge as it always has done.

In midnights of November,
When Dead Man's Fair is nigh,
And danger in the valley,
And anger in the sky,

Around the huddling homesteads
The leafless timber roars,
And the dead call the dying
And finger at the doors.

Oh, yonder faltering fingers
Are hands I used to hold;
Their false companion drowses
And leaves them in the cold.

Oh, to the bed of ocean,
To Africk and to Ind,
I will arise and follow
Along the rainy wind.

The night goes out and under
With all its train forlorn;
Hues in the east assemble
And cocks crow up the morn.

The living are the living
And dead the dead will stay,
And I will sort with comrades
That face the beam of day.

LP XIX

Chapter Five

To Ludlow

The lads in their hundreds to Ludlow come in for the fair,
There's men from the barn and the forge and the mill and the fold,
The lads for the girls and the lads for the liquor are there,
And there with the rest are the lads that will never be old.

There's chaps from the town and the field and the till and the cart,
And many to count are the stalwart, and many the brave,
And many the handsome of face and the handsome of heart,
And few that will carry their looks or their truth to the grave.

I wish one could know them, I wish there were tokens to tell
The fortunate fellows that now you can never discern;
And then one could talk with them friendly and wish them farewell
And watch them depart on the way that they will not return.

But now you may stare as you like and there's nothing to scan;
And brushing your elbow unguessed-at and not to be told
They carry back bright to the coiner the mintage of man,
The lads that will die in their glory and never be old.

ASL XXIII

To Ludlow -
The Fair, The Chimes, The Beer,
The Market, The Gallows

Much has been written and said of Ludlow's incomparable architecture and of the town's sublime setting.

A planned Norman town, with a parish church of cathedral-like proportions and a castle set high on rocks above the convergence of the Rivers Corve and Teme, Ludlow guards the mid-border lands of England and Wales known as the Welsh Marches. The entrances to the town are noble, with wide roads which sweep up to the old town's central heart. One of the town's original seven gateways survives and a large section of the town is still enfolded by the sandstone medieval walls that once guarded its townsfolk.

Much history has been made here. The Mortimers of Wigmore, "Not we of Kings, but Kings of us" their bold motto, held Ludlow castle and ruled England. Those who lived and governed from here fill the pages of Shakespeare's histories. Henry VIII's fives court is still standing here, his brother the Prince of Wales, Prince Arthur died here. The pomegranate, symbol of the House of Aragon, is carved in the Chapel walls, in celebration of Katherine of Aragon's union with Prince Arthur and not her later, more fateful marriage to Henry. The Lancastrian Princes Edward and Richard had their last days of quiet in Ludlow. They were both taken from the town in 1483 for Edward V's coronation and to their untimely deaths in the Tower.

The town is filled with buildings of high architectural merit; visually Ludlow is a delight and it is surrounded by countryside that rolls right up to the town walls. It is a special place and rightly acknowledged as such by the nation's leading architectural historians.

During the middle ages and through until the Jacobean era Ludlow was an administrative centre of much strategic importance as the capital of the Marches. The Normans had chosen a gracious yet clever spot on which to build a major settlement. The Corve valley's convergence with the River Teme forms a gorge-like setting as the Teme curls around the west and south of the town. From the Whitcliffe set high above Ludlow a glorious panorama of the old town centre is spread out and the scene is framed with the two Clee hills of Titterstone and Brown Clee. From here Ludlow indeed appears as the noble capital and stronghold it once was.

But what of Housman's Ludlow? From documents we know that Housman knew the town.
"I know Ludlow" he wrote in a letter to Maurice Pollet on 5 February 1933. In the collected verse which he called A Shropshire Lad, Ludlow becomes the undisputed capital, both geographically and spiritually, of the work. Housman's lad takes the Ludlow road - to come in for the fair and to drink his pints and quarts of Ludlow beer; he brings his flowers to sell at Ludlow's market; he walks out with Rose Harland on Sundays here, and in the week ploughs with his team beside the river bank at Ludlow. In Ludlow the luckless lad can get drunk, lose his sweetheart, or purchase a trifle at the May fair. Ludlow can also deal him the rougher cards of life. He can enlist here to leave by a road that he may not return.

There is much of Ludlow that Housman would recognise today. Certainly its streets and ancient buildings have survived with most of their original features intact. Amongst the more famous Ludlow landmarks there is the Castle, the gracious Broad Street, the half-timbered tracery of The Feathers Inn and the Parish Church with its magnificent tower, so often mentioned by Housman in his poems. The chimes that ring from the church tower, the May fair, the Monday market and rural life still dictate the pace of life here with chaps from the town and the field and the till and the cart.

From afar the town is still seen to be dominated by the tower of St Laurence's, Ludlow's magnificent parish church, and the castle. Twin symbols of medieval power - the church and the state. They also have much to symbolise of the fate that the Shropshire lad finds in Ludlow. Life and death is, after all, measured out between them.

Oh who is that young sinner with the handcuffs on his wrists?

And what has he been after that they groan and shake their fists?

And wherefore is he wearing such a conscience-stricken air?

Oh they're taking him to prison for the colour of his hair.

'Tis a shame to human nature, such a head of hair as his;

In the good old time 'twas hanging for the colour that it is;

Though hanging isn't bad enough and flaying would be fair

For the nameless and abominable colour of his hair.

Oh a deal of pains he's taken and a pretty price he's paid

To hide his poll or dye it of a mentionable shade;

But they've pulled the beggar's hat off for the world to see and stare,

And they're hailing him to justice for the colour of his hair.

Now 'tis oakum for his fingers and the treadmill for his feet

And the quarry-gang on Portland in the cold and in the heat,

And between his spells of labour in the time he has to spare

He can curse the God that made him for the colour of his hair.

AP XVIII

The building of the bell tower at St Laurence's is of a little more than passing church guide book reference. In 1433 the townspeople of Ludlow had finally decided that action should be taken against the Rector of the day, a John Donwode. The nature of their complaint was not only a lack of spiritual guidance from their priest, but of his neglect of the actual fabric and infrastructure of the church itself. Their petition was sent to the Pope in Rome who received their complaint with sympathy. As a result Donwode was pensioned off and a chaplain was sent from Rome to render better service to Ludlow's faithful. As a result, work was put in hand for the building of a bell tower, mainly due to the generosity of a bequest from a Richard Knyghtone, with further aid from Ludlow's rich and generous Palmers' Guild. The tower seems to have been completed, with bells installed, around the late 1460s.

The chimes of the tower, which are mentioned by Housman, seem to have been installed sometime in the early 17th century. We know that they were in existence by 1638 because the organist was paid 6s 8d (a large sum, it seems) to operate the chimes. Exactly as Housman recorded in his poem 'The conquering hero comes' is still played on Mondays, and every other day of the week has its own dedicated chime.

Yet more of Housman's spirit of Ludlow remains in the cycle of the rural year which still firmly influences the rhythm of the town. When so many other rural towns have lost their raison d'être and become commuter or totally tourist-lead communities, it is perhaps a remarkable feat that as we celebrate the centenary of the publication of A Shropshire Lad, those customs and practices which Housman noted in 1895 are still ongoing in Ludlow today, except it has to be said there is no longer a gallows!

Under the shadow of Ludlow tower, the lofty and majestic perpendicular bell tower which rises over the centre of St Laurence's, the parish church, the May fair is still held every year at May Day; on Monday the town is full and busy with buyers and sellers at the livestock market, the chimes of the tower still throw the quarters down on the streets and the chimes still play 'The conquering hero comes'.

So for those who come in search of the spirit of Ludlow which Housman captured so well, much is still left.

The Recruit

Leave your home behind, lad,
And reach your friends your hand,
And go, and luck go with you
While Ludlow tower shall stand.

Oh, come you home of Sunday
When Ludlow streets are still
And Ludlow bells are calling
To farm and lane and mill,

Or come you home of Monday
When Ludlow market hums
And Ludlow chimes are playing
'The conquering hero comes',

Come you home a hero,
Or come not home at all,
The lads you leave will mind you
Till Ludlow tower shall fall.

And you will list the bugle
That blows in lands of morn,
And make the foes of England
Be sorry you were born.

And you till trump of doomsday
On lands of morn may lie,
And make the hearts of comrades
Be heavy where you die.

Leave your home behind you,
Your friends by field and town:
Oh, town and field will mind you
Till Ludlow tower is down.

ASL III

It is often a favourite past-time here to recall the names and number of alehouses and inns that used to thrive in Ludlow. Indeed a former Ludlovian and publican, Harry Baker, was the author of 'An Alphabet of Ludlow Pubs'. Certainly in the 1920s and 1930s there were well over one hundred - and this for a town with a relatively small population which until very recently has remained static over the centuries. One of the main reasons for the multitude of these alehouses was the livestock market which attracted (as indeed it still does) large numbers of farmers selling their stock. Up until the mid-1950s, farmers were driving their livestock many miles on foot. I am told that the Corve Bridge and Lower Corve Street at the north end of the town (near the livestock market) would clatter to the sound of pigs, sheep, cattle and horses coming in. Many animals, including pigs and sheep, were shod to help them cope with the miles they had to travel to market, on hoof, of course!

Coming in to market was therefore a not inconsiderable social occasion. This was how news mainly got passed around scattered, remote communities. The well earned visit to the alehouse on market day was an all important part of the exchange of news. It was a long walk or ride home, or an even longer drive with sheep, cattle or pigs, and a top up at the inn would go a long way to smooth the journey. Ludlow was self-sufficient with breweries - it needed to be when ale houses on market days were open continuously and always full. There were consequently many breweries in Ludlow itself, keeping the town adequately provided for. A maltings still exists at the rear of one of the Corve Street properties. This in turn is opposite the site of one of the breweries; indeed much of Ludlow's brewing seems to have taken place in and around the Corve Street area.

"Ale, man, ale's the stuff to drink

For fellows whom it hurts to think:

Look into the pewter pot

To see the world as the world's not.

And faith, 'tis pleasant till 'tis past:

The mischief is that 'twill not last.

Oh I have been to Ludlow fair

And left my necktie God knows where,

And carried half-way home, or near,

Pints and quarts of Ludlow beer:

Then the world seemed none so bad,

And I myself a sterling lad;

And down in lovely muck I've lain,

Happy till I woke again."

from ASL LXII

Inns and alehouses flew under every banner from the Hop Pole to The Lamb; The Portcullis to The Nag's Head; joined with The Queen's Head, The Bell, The Wheatsheaf, The Star and Garter, The Ludlow Arms, The Charlton Arms, The Swan, The Stag, the Rose and Crown, The Church Inn, The New Inn, The Bull, The Bull Ring Tavern, The Raven, The Angel, The Horse and Jockey, the Half Moon and The Smithfield to name a mere few.

The cattlemarket in Corve Street has thrived on its present site for over 130 years. Before the coming of the railway to Ludlow it was down at the southern end of the town. Then, as now, its regular weekly market day was Monday when the town is filled with local farmers selling and many who now come from as far afield as Scotland and Kent to buy. Today, Ludlow is one of the five largest livestock markets in England. The market moved to its present site on the arrival of the railway to Ludlow.

The visitor who arrives by train today has no hesitation in recognising that they have arrived in a rural town dominated by the agricultural world which surrounds it. As the train pulls in to the station, there are the cattle pens, row after row - some open to the skies, some covered in Dutch barn-like structures. Then there is an apparently ramshackled corrugated iron and brick structure in the style of an early 1920's agricultural building. But seen and heard on market day, when it is crammed full of local farmers selling and folks from afar buying, and where a blink or a scratch of the eyelid may mark you down for 10 head of store cattle, it is a place of thriving economy for the area. And two more buildings dominate this very rural market town scene: the large red brick, but very handsome Victorian Marston's corn mill building to the left of the cattle market and then, as always in Ludlow, St Laurence's tower chiming the quarters and ringing the hours.*

Up hill from the station and cattle market runs the grand Corve Street with its strong Georgian facades, and behind the street and the cattle market twines Portcullis Lane, which once lead up to the town barn which stood at the top of the hill in the mid 18th century.

    * Author's note: Since writing, Ludlow livestock market has moved to the outskirts of the town. It is still held on a Monday.

When smoke stood up from Ludlow,
And mist blew off from Teme,
And blithe afield to ploughing
Against the morning beam
I strode beside my team,

The blackbird in the coppice
Looked out to see me stride,
And hearkened as I whistled
The trampling team beside,
And fluted and replied:

'Lie down, lie down, young yeoman;
What use to rise and rise?
Rise man a thousand mornings
Yet down at last he lies,
And then the man is wise.'

I heard the tune he sang me,
And spied his yellow bill;
I picked a stone and aimed it
And threw it with a will:
Then the bird was still.

Then my soul within me
Took up the blackbird's strain,
And still beside the horses
Along the dewy lane
It sang the song again:

'Lie down, lie down, young yeoman;
The sun moves always west;
The road one treads to labour
Will lead one home to rest,
And that will be the best.'

ASL VII

As Corve Street rises to the top of the hill on which the Normans built the town, it forms an area known as The Bull Ring. Here stands the celebrated Feathers Inn, a sublime example of Ludlow's half-timbered architecture. Opposite is the locally celebrated ironmongers, Rickards. Its galvanised watering cans hang over the door, forks for muck-spreading lean against the entrance, the prongs of the forks hung over with mole traps. Inside the air is a rural mixture of the horticultural potting compost, paraffin oil, and decades of dust from the wonderful, worn floor boards. The walls are lined with old wooden drawers, meticulously numbered perhaps sometime around the 30th year of Queen Victoria's reign, in which are secreted vine eyes, picture hooks, tilley lamp mantles, and staples and nails of every size. Rickards was established in Ludlow in 1864, and was one of many of its sort of which Ludlow was filled during Housman's lifetime. Rickards has endured; sadly many others have succumbed to the advent of the do-it-yourself warehouses and the greater mechanisation of the farmyard.

The Ludlow May fair has endured, though, and is still held in the heart of the town centre every year on 1st May. Originally, as with all rural towns, the May fair was a hireling fair. Agricultural labourers would come in with the tools of their trade to be hired by the bailiffs of the landowners for another year. It was a vital part of rural life. From Norman times onwards there were, of course, many fairs held in Ludlow. There were fairs held on the patron saint's day of the parish church - St Laurence's Day for instance; and many others granted by royal charter. A fair then was the life and breath of the economics of the town.

During the last century, a whole series of fairs were held in the South Shropshire area during May. Ludlow, as the largest settlement, was always the first fair to be held and was always the most important. There then followed fairs at Bishop's Castle, Clun and Craven Arms on 24th May. The Bishop's Castle fair was, even in the years up to the Second World War, still being held conjointly as a commercial fair for hiring labourers, selling stock and farm goods. However, the real commercial fair was brought to an abrupt end when a tractor pulling one of the booths for the pleasure fair ran over a cow!

Inevitably, as agricultural practices changed dramatically in the last quarter of the 19th century, so the more pleasurable aspects of the fair became predominant. Photographs taken at the time of the publication of A Shropshire Lad show glorious helter-skelters alongside the more traditional ribbon, lace and cloth sellers. And of course, the lads came in for the girls and the beer!

When first my way to fair I took

Few pence in purse had I,

And long I used to stand and look

At things I could not buy.

Now times are altered: if I care

To buy a thing, I can;

The pence are here and here's the fair,

But where's the lost young man?

To think that two and two are four

And neither five nor three

The heart of man has long been sore

And long 'tis like to be.

LPXXXV

Today there remains much of the spirit captured by Housman in his description of the roads to Ludlow carrying folks in for the fair. In the early evening on those first days of May the crowds approach The Bull Ring, or from the opposite side of town from the Broadgate. The throngs are carried along with the buoyancy and spirit of another spring and another fair time in Ludlow. It is still eagerly anticipated by the lads from the farms of today.

Housman's Ludlow also had its more serious side. Housman makes reference on several occasions to the gallows, and there was a gallows at Ludlow. From the town's earliest days there were many secure places to hold prisoners - the Castle itself held many prisoners throughout its history, but the town's system of portcullis gates linked by the high town walls also had their dark, damp dungeons. Ludlow's jail was at Ludford, just beyond the town immediately over the other side of the river at Ludford Bridge. A formidably beautiful building, it is today a glorious private residence.

When I came last to Ludlow

Amidst the moonlight pale,

Two friends kept step beside me,

Two honest lads and hale.

Now Dick lies long in the churchyard,

And Ned lies long in jail,

And I come home to Ludlow

Amidst the moonlight pale.

ASL LVIII

Ludlow was formally self-sufficient in its system of law. There were many Justice of the Peace who had power to sentence deportations or to pronounce the death sentence. Many dispensed these sentences from their own stately dining rooms, such as Justice Powell of Sutton Court in Corvedale who in the 18th century sentenced one of the local female tenants to deportation to Australia for stealing flax.

Ludlow's court room of today, and of yesterday, is in Mill Street. The building dates back to the 13th century (we know that it was in use as a guild hall by 1283). It is, as are most of Ludlow's ancient buildings, of great architectural as well as historical merit. It was the former medieval hall of Ludlow's powerful Palmers' Guild, who did much socially, administratively and ecclesiastically in Ludlow. They put much finance towards the building of St Laurence's, for instance.   The Guildhall at Ludlow has been in use as a court of justice for five centuries. Today, its outer appearance is that of a Georgian facade of the 1770s. Inside, its medieval ancient oak pillars are encased from floor to ceiling level by Gothic columns, but its great medieval beams arching the court room ceiling are still visible. It is an extremely gracious and elegant court room, with its Georgian modernisations now painted in a Wedgewood blue and white.

Of fatal justice meted out, Ludlow saw much. The site of the gallows was to the south-east of the town on a sharp rise of ground still called "Gallows Bank" today. It is the tract of green field which one can see from the town centre at the point where Brand Lane crosses over Broad Street. The end of the vision seen from Brand Lane is ultimately framed by Titterstone Clee, but the land in the near foreground is Gallows Bank. The condemned were led beyond the town walls through Galdeford Gate, and down hill along the former Over Galdeford - today's Lower Galdeford. They then passed uphill again onto Gallows Bank itself.

From Gallows Bank the prisoner could behold the power and might of the state and laws which had condemned him symbolised on the skyline of the town before him. The Castle, the southern streets with their great gates and portcullis ready to fall, all sweeping down to the river below it and the tower of St Laurence's dominating all, casting its shadow like a sun dial. Once its great bell had sounded the hour, the noose was drawn and the rope fell.

Eight O'Clock

He stood, and heard the steeple
Sprinkle the quarters on the morning town.
One, two, three, four, to market-place and people
It tossed them down.

Strapped, noosed, nighing his hour,
He stood and counted them and cursed his luck;
And then the clock collected in the tower
Its strength, and struck.

LP XV

It was underneath the shadow of Ludlow tower that A E Housman's ashes were finally laid to rest. He died, aged 77, on 30 April 1936. A funeral service becoming the classical scholar and the Kennedy Professor of Latin of Trinity College, Cambridge was held at Trinity College Chapel. Housman's coffin bore a wreath of laurel and bay from his family over which had been strewn boughs of white cherry blossom, a gesture and tribute to the author of 'Loveliest of Trees' which he would surely have appreciated.

Following cremation, his ashes were finally brought back to Shropshire, his land of lost content. They are laid within the north wall of Ludlow's parish church, St Laurence's, below the great perpendicular bell tower. His memorial tablet faces out to the north-west, the horizon bordered by Wenlock Edge and the hills which look west towards Clun. The sun sets on its course over these hills and as it sinks low in the western sky at certain times in summer, shines directly through opposite windows of Ludlow tower, radiating the sandstone walls with a golden glow. Where else should the poet of A Shropshire Lad find rest and peace but within these walls, and what ancient Shropshire hills should his memorial eternally look upon, but these?

In Memory of Alfred Edward Housman MA Oxon

Kennedy Professor of Latin
And Fellow of Trinity College
In the University of Cambridge

Author of A Shropshire Lad

Born 26 March 1859
Died 30 April 1936

"Good-night; ensured release,
Imperishable peace,
Have these for yours"

The final words quoted are Housman's own, taken from his own poem, 'Parta Quies'.

And so today, at 8.00 in the morning, 12 noon, 4 o'clock in the afternoon and finally at 8 o'clock in the evening, the chimes play from the tower. The bells then strike the hours and the quarters; those lads still come in for the May fair each year; the market on Monday thrives, and the orchards around renew their blossom each spring.

Parta Quies

Good-night; ensured release,
Imperishable peace,
Have these for yours,
While sea abides, and land,
And earth's foundations stand,
And heaven endures.

When earth's foundations flee,
Nor sky nor land nor sea
At all is found,
Content you, let them burn:
It is not your concern;
Sleep on, sleep sound.

MP XLVIII

The First of May

The orchards half the way
From home to Ludlow fair
Flowered on the first of May
In Mays when I was there;
And seen from stile or turning
The plume of smoke would show
Where fires were burning
That went out long ago.

Between the trees in flower
New friends at fairtime tread
The way where Ludlow tower
Stands planted on the dead.
Our thoughts, a long while after,
They think, our words they say;
Theirs now's the laughter,
The fair, the first of May.

The plum broke forth in green,
The pear stood high and snowed,
My friends and I between
Would take the Ludlow road;
Dressed to the nines and drinking
And light in heart and limb,
And each chap thinking
The fair was held for him.

Ay, yonder lads are yet
The fools that we were then;
For oh, the sons we get
Are still the sons of men.
The sumless tale of sorrow
Is all unrolled in vain:
May comes to-morrow
And Ludlow fair again.

LP XXXIV

Clun Castle

Chapter Six

The Westland

Clunton, Clunbury,
Clungunford and Clun,
Are the quietest places
Under the sun.

In valleys of springs of rivers,
By Ony and Teme and Clun,
The country for easy livers,
The quietest under the sun.

We still had sorrows to lighten,
One could not be always glad,
And lads knew trouble at Knighton
When I was a Knighton lad.

By bridges that Thames runs under,
In London, the town built ill,
'Tis sure small matter for wonder
If sorrow is with one still.

And if as a lad grows older
The troubles he bears are more,
He carries his griefs on a shoulder
That handselled them long before.

Where shall one halt to deliver
This luggage I'd lief set down?
Not Thames, not Teme is the river,
Nor London nor Knighton the town.

'Tis a long way further than Knighton,
A quieter place than Clun,
Where doomsday may thunder and lighten
And little 'twill matter to one.

ASL L

The Westland - Clunton, Clunbury, Clungunford and Clun

How can it be that a transition may be at once sudden but gradual, a change imperceptible but at once recognisable? Such changes occur with a masterly stroke at the hand of a masterly composer. And so it is on the westward road to Clun.

The rich, arable, undulating land of South Shropshire hardly seems to alter along the road to Clun but suddenly it appears that the hills have changed shape and the valleys are a little different. The long wood-clothed ridges of the valleys which converge around the Teme at Ludlow have become more rotund, somewhat dumpy and are like Christmas puddings in shape. Many are lined on their summits with trees that crown the ridge like tiaras, with trees radiating in gentle, carefully placed stages across the brow instead of diamonds. The hedgerows of the fields along their lower slopes (for their tops are becoming bare upland) run across these hillsides with the contour of the hills. Whereas the hedgerows of the Corvedale valleys run from the top of the hills to the bottom, those of the Clun valley area give the appearance of running from side to side, like rings round a barrel.

And as the traveller reaches Clun and its uplands there is the ultimate transformation as the Welsh border is reached. The fertile verdant and green clay lands of Shropshire become the high, peat, granite and lonely heights of mid-Wales. The words of Gurnemanz to Parsifal as they move imperceptibly from the forest to the temple of the Holy Grail come to mind; "here time becomes space."

For Housman the final western horizon was a special vision. When he beheld "the blue remembered hills" from his childhood home at Bromsgrove and gazed westward to Shropshire, across whose horizon the sun always set, we see Housman as if bound in a reverie. His dream land of lost content was always this land across which the sun slowly faded to rest. There are many beautiful passages in his verse about the last light of day sinking over these western border lands as the sun disappears across the Welsh border. "The foot of twilight still Is stolen toward the western sill ...", "West and away the wheels of darkness roll", "Beyond the moor and mountain crest Comrade, look not on the west - The sun is down and drinks away From air and land the lees of day."

The night comes slowly on after the last of day, and for Housman it often symbolises the apocalyptic pale horse of death. This western border land for Housman is special and sacrosanct. Let me now take you on the final Shropshire road to Wales.

By shores and woods and steeples
Rejoicing hearts receive
Poured on a hundred peoples
The far-shed alms of eve.

Her hands are filled with slumber
For world-wide labourers worn;
Yet those are more in number
That know her not from morn.

Now who sees night for ever,
He sees no happier sight:
Night and no moon and never
A star upon the night.

MP XXXVIII

But before these Celtic uplands can be reached with their vast expanses of sky, clouds, emptiness and the voice of the skylark, a rather bizarre out-post has to be crossed. This out-post, which has a certain feel of some American 19th century staging post, is almost precisely just that. Craven Arms is not even a town really. Its heart once lay in the railway station, and that was how the town grew out of the former tiny hamlet of Newton, on the banks of the Onny, which was the nearest settlement to the famously glorious 12th century manor house, Stokesay. No great ancient market thrived here, no church commemorates a Norman manor. It is a far more convenient place from which to leave than to know one has arrived.

The railway station at Craven Arms was a junction of lines coming in from the Welsh towns of Builth Wells and Knighton and from England from Ludlow, Shrewsbury, Ironbridge and Bishop's Castle. It seems that the name of the station was taken from the Craven Arms Hotel which stands on the other junction of the town - the cross roads. Here the road which passes from Ludlow in the south to Shrewsbury in the north, crosses the other which branches east to Much Wenlock and the road west that leads to Clun.

A somewhat curious obelisk marking the miles to some far off towns guards the western road to Wales. Off and away and under the railway bridge the road of today crosses Watling Street, the Roman road of yesterday, and gently the road bends round into the Clun valley, and winds to and through the little village of Aston-on-Clun.

Clun Bridge

When green buds hang in the elm like dust

And sprinkle the lime like rain,

Forth I wander, forth I must,

And drink of life again.

Forth I must by hedgerow bowers

To look at the leaves uncurled,

And stand in the fields where cuckoo-flowers

Are lying about the world.

MP IX

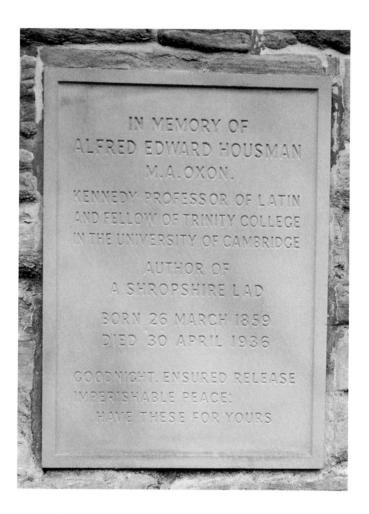

The Housman Memorial at St. Laurence's Parish Church, Ludlow.
Carved by Mr. Bill Griffin, stonemason, of Corve Street, Ludlow.

St. Laurence's Church, Ludlow - the Housman cherry tree.

True Marcher country. The final uplands of Shropshire's border with Wales; lonely uplands above Clun.

St. Swithun's churchyard, Clunbury, one of the quietest under the sun.
A group of Clun rams proving that this is the country for easy livers.

Aston-on-Clun still retains its character despite its overt prettiness. It is famous locally for keeping up an old local custom, of which something should be said before we journey through the village further into the west. Indeed it would not be possible to pass through Aston-on-Clun without seeing the rather gnarled tree in the village centre from which hang an array of flags. The colours of the flags are faded by degrees as the wind and the weather blow past them.

The flags used to be put up annually on 29 May to mark the wedding anniversary of two of the landed gentry who lived nearby. The flags would be left for a whole year and a whole new set would be put up on the next anniversary.

The custom was first started on 29 May 1786 when John Marston of the Hall at Aston-on-Clun married a Miss Mary Carter from Sibdon Castle, some two miles from the village. Locally it was a popular marriage, so in celebration the villagers at Aston dressed the tree that stood in the very middle of the village for all to see their affection. To demonstrate his regard for the the villagers, Mr Marston in turn gave the villagers a sovereign and off they all went to the inn - the Kangaroo Inn of today's village - to celebrate in grand style.

And so the tree has remained dressed to this day. The final flag to be nailed up is always held by a horse shoe. This can still be seen, as can a penny, also nailed into the tree. This was given by a woman who was walking through the Clun valley country villages selling lace. She mistakenly thought she had to pay to watch the ceremony, so the penny was ceremoniously nailed in thanks to the tree as well.

The workers of the Marston estate were still involved in the ceremony up until the 1950's. Today the flags are provided by the parish of Hopesay, to which Aston-on-Clun belongs. The Kangaroo Inn thrives and to sit around the bedecked tree on a summer's day, with little to think of and nowhere to go, seems not such a bad thing to do.

Think no more, lad; laugh, be jolly:

Why should men make haste to die?

Empty heads and tongues-a-talking

Make the rough road easy walking,

And the feather pate of folly

Bears the falling sky.

Oh, 'tis jesting, dancing, drinking

Spins the heavy world around.

If young hearts were not so clever,

Oh, they would be young for ever:

Think no more; 'tis only thinking

Lays lads underground.

ASL XLIX

The road westward from Aston-on-Clun goes forth down the wide and generous valley of the River Clun. Set right in the middle of the valley bottom lies Clunbury. From a distance its square church tower strikes an evocative form against bracken covered hillsides which enfold the little village. When the traveller takes the road from Wales into England, Clunbury displays all the characteristics which epitomise the quintessential English village. And I am here not about describing perhaps the vision the foreign traveller has of a rather polished Kent or Cotswold village, hanging baskets and gardens all meticulous and manicured. No. Clunbury is real! It is a working rural village with mud on the road borne from the agricultural world that surrounds it. It must be, for its church's dedicatee is St Swithun, so it is not guaranteed endless cloudless summer skies! Those famous Welsh mists close in quickly here for the border is not far off.

Clunbury has a solid ancient church with a classically romantic graveyard full of interesting tombs and headstones, yew trees and in the summer foams with the white cow parsley blossoms. It has a river running through the centre of the village (the River Clun, of course), complete with a wooden footbridge. In the orchard next to the churchyard the sheep are very literally safely grazing. The houses are all different shapes and sizes but all in vernacular style, all of architectural interest but very much lived in by their owners who live and work in the area. Its remoteness from the main arterial roads, distance from large towns and seclusion from the second home property speculator has left it intact and in peace.

Oh stay at home, my lad, and plough

The land and not the sea,

And leave the soldiers at their drill,

And all about the idle hill

Shepherd your sheep with me.

Oh stay with company and mirth

And daylight and the air;

Too full already is the grave

Of fellows that were good and brave

And died because they were.

LP XXXVIII

This quietness and sense of well being led the inhabitants of the area to compose their own little verse about their homeland. It is the much quoted, and often wrongly attributed to A E Housman, "Clunton and Clunbury, Clungunford and Clun Are the quietest places under the sun". Housman did, of course, choose to quote these anonymous local lines at the beginning of his poem "In valleys of springs of rivers". This little jingle has been quoted to me by Shropshire folk with a couple of variants. It was recited to me in the 1960's with the word "sleepiest" as the favourite form and "drunkenest" when in more spirited vein. Housman had obviously heard this version too, for he wrote "The stanza prefixed to no. L of A Shropshire Lad is traditional. One version is "drunkenest". I have also come across another local rhyme which links it with the "drunkenest places under the sun". These lines ran "Before my day is done, I'll go and share the vices Of Clungunford and Clun, And watch the red sun sinking Across the March again." This verse was even quoted, apparently, many, many years ago, by a former Bishop of Hereford giving evidence to the Licensing Commission.

As in Corvedale, this area too had its cider houses, as might be understood from these local ditties. As always in remote location in days of poor communications these houses served several purposes, the two uppermost needs serving as place to meet one's neighbours for the sake of sheer enjoyment and the second, important function of being places to catch up with local and national news. But on this remoter western road to Clun and Knighton, they had served another function.

The Ludlow area with the richer Corvedale lands served, and still serves, to fatten the livestock brought down from the higher grounds where grass is sparse and winters are even harsher. Ludlow with its livestock market was a main trading centre and the other busy and big market was at Knighton. Knighton's market still thrives today and for the same reasons. The Welsh border hill farmers would sell their stock to be fattened in the Ludlow area. In Housman's Shropshire Lad's day, as it had been for centuries, the big trade and movement was in sheep. It was a two day walk from Ludlow to Knighton with a flock of sheep, and there were well known and defined places to stop. These were alehouses or cider houses where the shepherd and his sheep could both rest! My old friends who walked from Corvedale to Knighton with their sheep would know where they might stop out under the stars for the night safely. Sometimes, an inn or cider house gave over a field for the shepherd to keep his sheep for the night. The way from Corvedale to Knighton lay through Clungunford and Leintwardine and west into Knighton along the Teme valley. Livestock was still being driven on foot through this route until the late 1940's.

The other route between Knighton and Clun lay across high, undulating moorland and was lonely for the shepherd. This drovers road crossed the Shropshire borderland at an altitude of over 1,200 feet and here the shepherd tried to sleep out with little cover at night. Above him though, in the darkness, the planets and galaxies and constellations which he would know well, glittered down through clear, cold skies. Perhaps he mused on the changing fortune of his friend lying in Shrewsbury jail.

On moonlit heath and lonesome bank

The sheep beside me graze;

And yon the gallows used to clank

Fast by the four cross ways.

A careless shepherd once would keep

The flocks by moonlight there,

And high amongst the glimmering sheep

The dead man stood on air.

They hang us now in Shrewsbury jail:

The whistles blow forlorn,

And trains all night groan on the rail

To men that die at morn.

There sleeps in Shrewsbury jail to-night,

Or wakes, as may betide,

A better lad, if things were right,

Than most that sleep outside.

And naked to the hangman's noose

The morning clocks will ring

A neck God made for other use

Than strangling in a string.

And sharp the link of life will snap,

And dead on air will stand

Heels that held up as straight a chap

As treads upon the land.

So here I'll watch the night and wait

To see the morning shine,

When he will hear the stroke of eight

And not the stroke of nine;

And wish my friend as sound a sleep

As lads' I did not know,

That shepherded the moonlit sheep

A hundred years ago.

ASL IX

As the shepherd or traveller approached Clun westward from Clunbury, they would notice that again, almost imperceptibly, the landscape and the former wide valley bottom had changed. At Clunton the hills are closing in, Radnor Wood and Clunton Hill from the north, and the darker Sowdley Wood and the Black Hill to the south. As one stops to look and breathe in the air, the atmosphere is changing too. The hills are pent-in. The area has long been known to man. A mile and half climb north from Clunton leads to Bury Ditches, a high impressive Iron Age fort of commanding situation and vision. Parts of its hillside stand in the bracing wind which blows in from Wales across the high uplands of the Clun Forest. The area is thick with tumuli and earthworks of the Iron Age period. Man came here early to these cloud driven heights but now man has left them for the valleys and deserted these now empty border fortresses.

Clun Castle

Westward on the high-hilled plains

Where for me the world began,

Still, I think, in newer veins

Frets the changeless blood of man.

Now that other lads than I

Strip to bathe on Severn shore,

They, no help, for all they try,

Tread the mill I trod before.

There, when hueless is the west

And the darkness hushes wide,

Where the lad lies down to rest

Stands the troubled dream beside.

There, on thoughts that once were mine,

Day looks down the eastern steep,

And the youth at morning shine

Makes the vow he will not keep.

ASL LV

Clun was properly settled and firmly established by man as a town at the end of the 10th century. The Norman, Picot de Say built his castle fortress on the raised ground on the north banks of the River Clun. The Norman building was never really developed and it stands alone, a rather lonely and sad monument guarding sheep and the pretty water ways of this breach in the hills and twist of the river. The town was settled, and Doomsday records that there were 183 burgage plots in Clun in the 11th century. The river has always flowed through here and an intricate, delicate and narrow five-arched medieval bridge carries the traveller to a choice of ancient roadways. Onwards west and the road traverses through a ravishing and dramatic valley past the historically interesting Lower Spoad Farm. At the farm is a carved wooden mantelpiece over one of the fireplaces. It depicts a hunter aiming his arrows at a fleeing deer and, despite being in a house of the 16th century, has been attributed to Norman origin. The former ancient boundary dug for King Offa, to separate Saxon and Celt, is also crossed at Lower Spoad. This road continues past Hall of the Forest an evocative name for an old 16th century house built by one of the local border Marchers, the FitzAlans. The road yet winds up to the heights of Clun Forest and the Kerry Hills who have both given their names to the famous sheep of Shropshire - inheritors and inhabitants of these hills. Finally the border of today is reached near the Anchor Inn, and the last house in England, virtually at the very summit of the Kerry Hills. The summit is known as Kerry Pole. Gone is the green grass filled with clover, gone the red clay of the sandstone lands, gone the leafy woods. The margin of Housman's sunset falls here.

The other road south-west from Clun takes off across more high ground to the old border town of Knighton where the Welsh border is defined by the River Teme. Offa's Dyke is here too and crossed the land north to south. The road east from Knighton will lead down the Teme valley to Ludlow; through orchards, past farms, past spires; a happy highway.

The road north-west back over the high deserted ground leads to Clun again, past three lonely cross-roads at Five Turnings, New Invention and Rockhill and down into Clun. The air is fresh here and does not confuse the senses. The two roads from Knighton to Clun and Ludlow define the choices of life for Housman and his Shropshire Lad. The road that leads one home will always be the best. The difficult, lonely road which is taken in darkness is brim full of sadness.

Up at the three crossways the wind blows from the west. As the sun sets beyond the Welsh hills a rose pink glow settles on these Shropshire hill tops and the wind is still. In mid-summer, light lingers here past the hour of eleven in the evening, and then night slowly covers the land. The moon will rise, but be low over Wenlock Edge and the Clee Hills. The little thin ribbon of road leading down to Clun will be white, always leading one west.

White in the moon the long road lies,

The moon stands blank above;

White in the moon the long road lies

That leads me from my love.

Still hangs the hedge without a gust,

Still, still the shadows stay:

My feet upon the moonlit dust

Pursue the ceaseless way.

The world is round, so travellers tell,

And straight though reach the track,

Trudge on, trudge on, 'twill all be well,

The way will guide one back.

But ere the circle homeward hies

Far, far must it remove:

White in the moon the long road lies

That leads me from my love.

ASL XXXVI

The farms of home lie lost in even,
I see far off the steeple stand;
West and away from here to heaven
Still is the land.

There if I go no girl will greet me,
No comrade hollo from the hill,
No dog run down the yard to meet me:
The land is still.

The land is still by farm and steeple,
And still for me the land may stay:
There I was friends with perished people,
And there lie they.

MP XIV

The Poems of A E Housman quoted in The Land of Lost Content

Index by first line of Poem

Throughout the book, A E Housman's poems are quoted as ASL, LP, MP and AP and refer to A Shropshire Lad, Last Poems, More Poems and Additional Poems respectively. The Roman numerals refer to the number of the poems as they appear in complete editions.

Suggested Further Reading

The Collected Poems of A E Housman
Published by Jonathan Cape

A E Housman Collected Poems and Selected Prose
Edited by Christopher Ricks; Published by Penguin Books

A E Housman
by Keith Jebb; Published by Border Lines

(At the time of going to press, several biographies of Housman are currently
out of print but are often available in second-hand bookshops.
The classics are by Richard Graves and Norman Page)

Shropshire Seasons
by Gordon Dickins; Published by Shropshire Books

Walks With Writers
by Gordon Dickins and Gladys Mary Coles; Published by Shropshire Books
(includes walks in the Shropshire countryside amongst the places of Housman's poems)

More books on Shropshire's literature and countryside published by Shropshire Books:

An Illustrated Literary Guide to Shropshire Gordon Dickins	£5.50
Walks With Writers Gordon Dickins and Gladys Mary Coles	£3.50
Shropshire From The Air Michael Watson and Chris Musson	£13.99
Shropshire Seasons Gordon Dickins	£14.99
The Shropshire Severn Edited by Richard Morriss	£14.99

For a complete list of Shropshire Books titles
please contact:

Shropshire Books
Information & Community Services
Column House
7 London Road
Shrewsbury SY2 6NW.